HOTSPOTS
MALTA

Thomas Cook

D0995801

Written by Paul Murphy, updated by David Browne

Published by Thomas Cook Publishing
A division of Thomas Cook Tour Operations Limited
Company Registration no. 1450464 England
The Thomas Cook Business Park, Unit 9, Coningsby Road,
Peterborough PE3 8SB, United Kingdom
Email: sales@thomascook.com, Tel: + 44 (0) 1733 416477
www.thomascookpublishing.com

Produced by Cambridge Publishing Management Limited
Burr Elm Court, Main Street, Caldecote CB23 7NU

ISBN: 978-1-84157-858-3

First edition © 2006 Thomas Cook Publishing
This second edition © 2008
Text © Thomas Cook Publishing
Maps © Thomas Cook Publishing/PCGraphics (UK) Limited

Series Editor: Diane Ashmore
Production/DTP Editor: Steven Collins

Printed and bound in Spain by GraphyCems

Cover photography © Thomas Cook

Although every care has been taken in compiling this publication, and the contents
are believed to be correct at the time of printing, Thomas Cook Tour Operations
Limited cannot accept any responsibility for errors or omission, however caused,
or for changes in details given in the guidebook, or for the consequences of any
reliance on the information provided. Descriptions and assessments are based on
the author's views and experiences when writing and do not necessarily represent
those of Thomas Cook Tour Operations Limited.

CONTENTS

INTRODUCTION 5
Getting to know Malta 8
The best of Malta 10
Symbols key 12

RESORTS 13
Sliema 15
St Julian's & Paceville 20
Bugibba & Qawra 24
St Paul's Bay 28
Mellieha 32

EXCURSIONS 37
Valletta 39
The Three Cities 51
Medieval Mdina 56
Rabat 62
Gozo 67
Comino 77
Malta panorama 78
Mediterranean cruise 83
The Blue Grotto & the
    south-west 86
Wine tourism 90

LIFESTYLE 93
Food & drink 95
Menu decoder 98
Shopping 100
Children 102
Sports & activities 104
Festivals & events 106

PRACTICAL INFORMATION 109
Accommodation 110
Preparing to go 113
During your stay 117

INDEX 125

MAPS
Malta 6–7
Sliema 14
St Julian's & Paceville 21
Valletta 38
The Three Cities 50
Mdina 58
Gozo 66

WHAT'S IN YOUR GUIDEBOOK?

Independent authors Impartial up-to-date information from our travel experts who meticulously source local knowledge.

Experience Thomas Cook's 165 years in the travel industry and guidebook publishing enriches every word with expertise you can trust.

Travel know-how Contributions by thousands of staff around the globe, each one living and breathing travel.

Editors Travel-publishing professionals, pulling everything together to craft a perfect blend of words, pictures, maps and design.

You, the traveller We deliver a practical, no-nonsense approach to information, geared to how you really use it.

▶ *Alexandra Pace, Valletta*

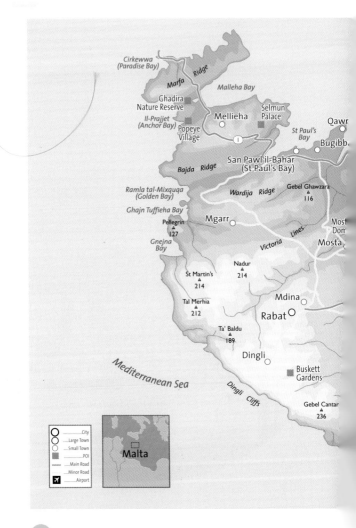

Cirkewwa
(Paradise Bay)

Marfa Ridge

Malleha Bay

Ghadira
Nature Reserve

Il-Prajjet
(Anchor Bay)

Popeye
Village

Mellieha

Selmun
Palace

Qawr

St Paul's
Bay

Bugibb

San Pawl il-Bahar
(St Paul's Bay)

Bajda Ridge

Ramla tal-Mixquqa
(Golden Bay)

Wardija Ridge

Gebel Ghawzara
▲
116

Ghajn Tuffieha Bay

Pellegrin
▲
127

Mgarr

Victoria Lines

Most
Dom

Mosta

Gnejna
Bay

Nadur
▲
214

St Martin's
▲
214

Tal Merhia
▲
212

Mdina

Rabat

Ta' Baldu
▲
189

Dingli

Mediterranean Sea

Dingli Cliffs

Buskett
Gardens

Gebel Cantar
▲
236

○ .....City
◎ .....Large Town
○ .....Small Town
■ .....POI
─ .....Main Road
.....Minor Road
✈ .....Airport

Malta

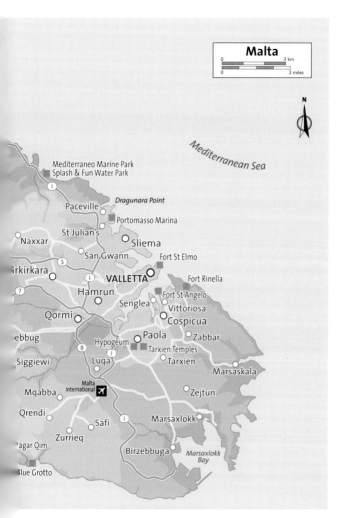

Getting to know Malta

The Maltese islands form an archipelago in the middle of the Mediterranean. Malta is the largest of the group and by far the most popular as a holiday destination with well-developed modern resorts, harbours suitable for yachts and cruise liners and an international airport. Its sister island to the north, Gozo, is smaller, more rural and less developed as a holiday island but has its own attractions that make it worth a visit. In between is the tiny island of Comino which has a population of less than ten and one hotel that is open only during the summer. There are several uninhabited islands: Cominotto next to Comino; Filfla, a rocky outcrop off the southern coast of Malta; and St Paul's islands just off the coast at St Paul's Bay in the north-east. Malta is about the size of the Isle of Wight, measuring 21 km (13 miles) long by 14 km (9 miles) wide at its furthest points. Gozo is just 14 km (9 miles) by 6.5 km (4 miles).

The British love affair with Malta goes back over 200 years when a naval force led by Horatio Nelson liberated the island from the tyranny of Napoleon. The British were an integral part of Maltese life from 1800 to 1979 and British influences are still visible. Most Maltese speak English fluently. Malta gained its independence in 1964 but remains a member of the Commonwealth. It is now also a member state of the European Union with the euro as its currency.

Although Malta is famous today as a laid-back sunshine holiday destination it has a turbulent history. Not just once, but twice, events on this tiny rock have shaped the course of world history. First was the Great Siege of Malta in 1565, when Malta became the decisive battleground in the conflict between Islam and Christianity. A force of 40,000 Turks fought the Maltese defenders and the Crusader Knights of St John, who had made Malta their base. After huge losses on both sides, the Ottoman Empire was defeated. Such was the gratitude of the Pope and European kings that Malta was rewarded with riches that helped endow Malta with the country churches and official buildings that are still very much in evidence today. Its second period of strategic significance was during World War II, when its geographical position made it the focal point of Mediterranean and North African conflicts. It endured 154 days and nights of Blitz, and was recorded as the most bombed place on earth. But the islanders were resilient and Malta continued to operate as a vital supply point for Allied convoys. Britain awarded the island, and by implication every islander, the George Cross, the highest award for civilian gallantry.

⬥ *Azure Window, Gozo*

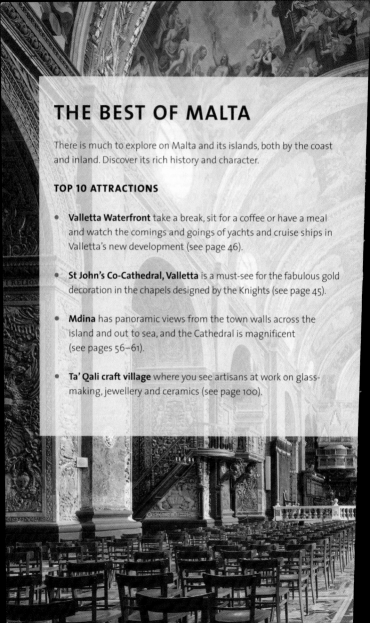

THE BEST OF MALTA

There is much to explore on Malta and its islands, both by the coast and inland. Discover its rich history and character.

TOP 10 ATTRACTIONS

- **Valletta Waterfront** take a break, sit for a coffee or have a meal and watch the comings and goings of yachts and cruise ships in Valletta's new development (see page 46).

- **St John's Co-Cathedral, Valletta** is a must-see for the fabulous gold decoration in the chapels designed by the Knights (see page 45).

- **Mdina** has panoramic views from the town walls across the island and out to sea, and the Cathedral is magnificent (see pages 56–61).

- **Ta' Qali craft village** where you see artisans at work on glass-making, jewellery and ceramics (see page 100).

- **Boat ride** No visit to Malta is complete without a boat ride, preferably in a glass-bottomed boat (see page 85).

- **Gozo** The island that is so relaxed that people say time stands still (see page 67).

- **Portomaso** Wander around St Julian's and Paceville's luxury marina and residential development (see page 20).

- **Diving Malta** has at least 25 safe diving sites, including shipwrecks, with diving centres catering for all levels of diver (see pages 16, 24, 34).

- **Mosta Dome** Marvel at the magnificent Mosta Dome, reputed to be the third-largest unsupported dome in Europe (see page 78).

- **The Malta Experience** This audio-visual spectacular in Mdina is an entertaining introduction to the history of Malta (see page 42).

The highly decorated interior of St John's Co-Cathedral, Valletta

SYMBOLS KEY

The following symbols are used throughout this book:

ⓐ address   ☏ telephone   ⓕ fax   ⓦ website address   ⓔ email
🕓 opening times   ❶ important

The following symbols are used on the maps:

🛈	information office	⭕	city
✉	post office	⬤	large town
🛍	shopping	○	small town
🛫	airport	◼	POI (point of interest)
✚	hospital	▦	motorway
⛨	police station	—	main road
🚌	bus station	—	minor road
✝	church		
❶	numbers denote featured cafés, restaurants & evening venues		

RESTAURANT CATEGORIES
The symbol after the name of each restaurant listed in this guide
indicates the price of a typical three-course meal without drinks
for one person:
£ up to €5   ££ €5–€10   £££ over €10

◗ *Malta is full of history, like the church in Balzan*

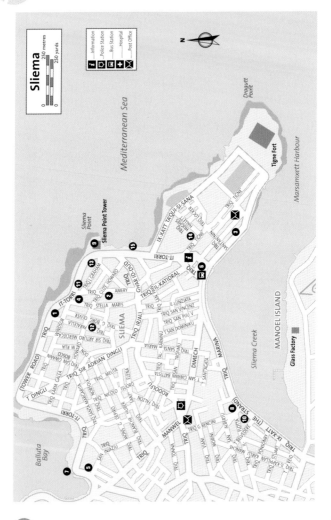

Sliema

Sliema (pronounced 'Slee-ma') is the fashionable part of Malta, with fine shopping, dining and top-class hotels. It is not only a popular resort but a much sought-after place to live. An address in Sliema has class and a price tag to go with it.

The town is built on a headland and has two waterfronts, one facing out to the Mediterranean Sea and the other facing Valletta across Marsamxett Harbour with Manoel Island, home of the Malta Yacht Club, in between. It's from here that most island boat cruises start, at jetties all along The Strand and Tigne Seafront. From here you can catch buses to Valletta and most other parts of the island. The Tigne peninsula, which juts out pointing towards Valletta, has good places for swimming but there is no beach.

The northern waterfront, Tower Road, has been developed into a charming, tree-lined promenade all the way to the neighbouring resort of St Julian's and you can find numerous cafés, bars and restaurants along its length. At the tip of the headland is Tigne Fort, the last of the defences built by the Knights in 1792.

Sliema's shopping centre is between the two waterfronts and you will find international stores such as Marks and Spencer and Stefanel as well as local independent shops and boutiques. Sliema's shops are among the best on the island – look for Maltese lace, fine silverware and pottery. From the Tigne Seafront there is a bridge over to Manoel Island where there is a glass-making factory operated by Phoenician Glassblowers: you can watch exquisite items being made and buy their products in a showroom.

Sliema is also the location of some fine hotels, including the 4-star Victoria Hotel and its new neighbour, The Palace, a 5-star establishment on the High Street. The neighbourhood has numerous attractive Art Nouveau villas built in the early 20th century for wealthy families who sought to break out of the confines of Valletta.

THINGS TO SEE & DO

Harbour tours

A cruise around Valletta and the Three Cities or the ferry across to Valletta is an indispensable part of anyone's visit to Malta. Boats depart regularly from The Strand. Enquire at the booths that line the promenade.

Diving

Aquanauts Dive School in the Qui Si Sana area of the seafront provides dive trips and diving courses. Their trial scuba dives are very popular with visitors and provide a perfect introduction to the underwater world.

ⓐ NSTS Aqua Centre, 60 IX Xatt, Sliema ⓣ 2131 9732
ⓦ www.maltascuba.com

Swimming

Sunbathing and swimming are 'on the rocks' at Sliema. The rocks are smooth and shelve gradually into the sea, running along the north side of the peninsula towards St Julian's Tower. There are public and private lidos along the Qui Si Sana and Tower Road, complete with cafés and watersports facilities.

SHOPPING

On Bisazza Street, pop in to the four-storey **Plaza Shopping Centre**. Here you will find the top international labels all under one roof. Open Mon–Sat 09.00–13.00 and 16.00–19.00.

Ginza Cute swimwear tops the fashions at this small corner boutique. ⓐ St Dominic Street ⓣ 2134 3359

Mil Ideas Jewellery, ceramics and stylishly designed household items are among the gifts to be found in this delightful shop.
ⓐ Along Tower Road ⓣ 2134 2266

TAKING A BREAK

Cara's Café £ ❶ A popular place for snacking on light meals and pastries and there can be long queues at weekends. The 'Sweets Gallery' is heaven for anyone with a sweet tooth, and you can sip on a yoghurt milkshake in any of 20 flavours. ⓐ 249 Tower Road, Sliema ⓣ 2134 3432

La Cuccagna £ ❷ Small, casual, family-run restaurant near the sea, serving pizzas and pasta. The ricotta-filled ravioli is home-made, as are the burgers. Gluten-free pasta and pizzas available at one day's notice. ⓐ 47 Amery Street, Sliema ⓣ 2134 6703 ⓔ adega@vol.net.mt

De Giorgio £ ❸ Specializes in Maltese food and pastries. ⓐ 17 Tigne Seafront, Sliema ⓣ 2134 6215

Surfside £ ❹ Though it looks like any other Tower Road beachside kiosk, the pizzas here are delicious and the crowd is usually very lively. Large terrace overlooking the sea. ⓐ Tower Road, opposite New Tower Palace Hotel ⓣ 2134 5384

AFTER DARK

Restaurants
Piccolo Padre £ ❺ Great little pizzeria in the basement of Barracuda (see below). Very lively – ideal for all ages. Book a seat with views on to Balluta Bay. ⓐ 195 Main Street, Balluta Bay ⓣ 2134 4875

Ta'Kris £ ❻ Locals say that 'Dad's Braggioli', made from thin slices of beef rolled and stuffed with minced pork and ham then braised slowly in a tomato and wine sauce, is as close as you can get to Maltese home cooking in a restaurant. ⓐ 80 Fawwara Lane, Sliema ⓣ 2133 7367

Barracuda ££ ❼ Excellent Italian restaurant, specialising in fish, occupying a sturdy 18th-century stone house on the edge of Balluta Bay.

⬤ *Promenade, Sliema*

Book a table with a waterside view. ⓐ 194 Main Street, Balluta Bay
ⓣ 2133 1817

Chez Philipe £target£ ⓪ On the border between Sliema and Gzira, this is a quirky eatery run by a Frenchman. The fare is French provincial; not fancy but wholesome and good. ⓐ 181 The Strand ⓣ 2133 0755

Divino ££ ❾ Located in the Fortizza Fort across a bridge over the moat, the restaurant is down a flight of stairs deep inside the fort. Contemporary styling with subdued lighting, and serving a range of Mediterranean dishes and Maltese specials and fresh fish. ⓐ Il-Fortizza, Tower Road, Sliema ⓣ 2133 2521

Krishna ££ ❿ Sliema's best Indian restaurant, with nice decor and some unusual offerings, such as almond fish and *palak gosht* (a spinach dish). ⓐ The Strand ☎ 2134 6291

Marianna's Tex-Mex Restaurant ££ ⓫ Bright Mexican prints and south-western kitsch adorn this delightful Mexican restaurant, which boasts the best margaritas on the island.
ⓐ 132 Tower Road, opposite the promenade ☎ 2131 8943

Ristorante Fumia ££ ⓬ A great seafood restaurant with a menu that varies according to catch brought in on the day. Regarded as one of the best in Sliema. ⓐ 16 High Street, Sliema ☎ 2131 9209

Ta'Kolina ££ ⓭ A favourite with locals, serving a mixture of Maltese and Italian dishes. Rabbit cooked in wine is a speciality. Portions are generous. ⓐ 151 Tower Road, Sliema ☎ 2133 5106

Nightlife
Frenchies Nightclub and Disco ⓮ Huge venue set in the rustic atmosphere of an old fortress, with a smaller club, **The Shelter**, tucked away within.
ⓐ Crowne Plaza Hotel ☎ 2132 3228 ⏰ From 21.00 Wed–Sun

Venus ⓯ This nightclub is the main entertainment venue in the Preluna Hotel and has a high-tech sound and light system, with live music at weekends. ⓐ 124 Tower Road, Sliema ☎ 2133 4001

PROMENADING
When the sun goes down local families come out – as they do all over the Mediterranean – for a *passegiata* (promenade), particularly along Tower Road. Stalls selling Maltese snacks and ice creams, and impromptu markets, are set up to catch the passing trade.

St Julian's & Paceville

St Julian's has grown from being a small, sheltered fishing village into one of Malta's biggest and busiest resorts. Fishing still goes on, and in Spinola Bay and St George's Bay the traditional brightly coloured fishing boats known as *luzzus* compete for space amongst pleasure craft.

The traditional centre of St Julian's is the area around Spinola Bay, Portomaso, which is now a smart yachting marina complex with a new Hilton Hotel and numerous up-market restaurants and bars. The area is dominated by the landmark Portomaso Tower, Malta's only skyscraper, an office block coloured in bold terracotta and deep blue.

Between Spinola Bay and St George's Bay is Paceville (pronounced parch-ay-vill), the nightlife capital of Malta, chock-a-block with bars and disco clubs. It seems quite mellow in the daytime, when most attention is paid to the Bay Street tourist complex, a multistorey shopping and entertainment centre. Most nights of the week, but especially at weekends, the area comes alive with loud music and is buzzing until the early hours with crowds of young people from all over the island.

At the northern end of St Julian's is St George's Bay, which has a small sandy beach and places to eat and drink in a more relaxed and quiet atmosphere. The hill beside the bay has several up-market hotel developments. At the tip of the headland is Dragonara Point, where Malta's largest casino is located in the Dragonara Palace, an ornate 19th-century mansion behind the Westin Dragonara Resort Hotel.

THINGS TO SEE & DO

Most sunbathing in the St Julian's area is done at lidos found along the coastline or around the pools within resort hotel complexes. One of the best lidos is the Reef Club, an exclusive beach club offering a selection of watersports, including waterskiing and windsurfing.

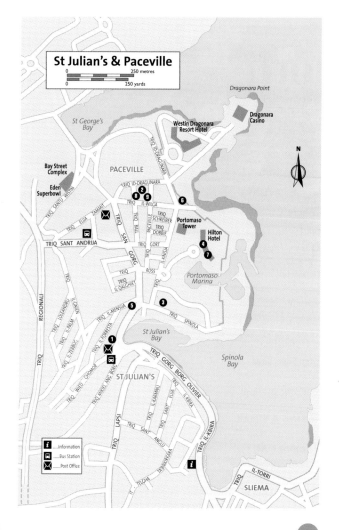

● *Spinola Bay, St Julian's*

Divewise

Scuba-diving school within the Westin Dragonara resort complex, with a waterfront location, and pools and sheltered areas where most of the training dives take place.

ⓘ 2135 6441 ⓦ www.divewise.com.mt ⓔ info@divewise.com.mt

Eden Superbowl

Tenpin bowling centre with 20 lanes.

ⓐ St George's Road, Paceville ⓘ 2371 0777 ⓔ superbowl@edenleisure.com

TAKING A BREAK

Il Kantina £ ❶ Rustic-style establishment in a busy location right at the head of Spinola Bay. ⓐ St George's Road ⓘ 2133 9865

Piece of Cake £ ❷ Popular café, serving enormous portions of cake and ice cream, plus snacks. ⓐ 23 Wilga Street, Paceville

AFTER DARK

Restaurants

Bouzouki £ ❸ Family-run Greek restaurant overlooking Spinola Bay, where the Meze portions are so generous you may not need a main course. ⓐ 135 Spinola Road, St Julian's ❶ 2138 7127

Buffalo Bill's ££ ❹ American themed steakhouse and a meat-eater's paradise. The bar area is done out like a cowboy saloon from a Hollywood film set but the tables on the terrace are more genuinely Mediterranean. ⓐ Portomaso Marina, St Julian's ❶ 2138 9290 ⓔ steakhouse@waldonet.mt

Dolce Vita ££ ❺ A fine restaurant specialising in seafood, and which overlooks the picturesque Spinola Bay. ⓐ 159 Triq San Gorg, St Julian's ❶ 2133 7036 ❶ From 18.00 daily

La Maltija ££ ❻ One of the few restaurants in the area serving only Maltese traditional food. The building is an old town house that used to be occupied by British officers serving in Malta. ⓐ 1 Church Street, Paceville ❶ 2135 9602 ⓦ www.lamaltija.com

Blue Elephant £££ ❼ Thai food served in the exotic surroundings of the Hilton Hotel, overlooking the Portomaso Marina. ⓐ Hilton Hotel, Portomaso ❶ 2138 3383

Nightlife

The Alley ❽ Paceville's oldest bar and very popular at weekends and on Wednesdays for rock music, with live bands occasionally. ⓐ Wilga Street, Paceville ❶ 2138 2979, 9988 1266 ⓦ www.alley.com.mt

Coconut Grove and Remedy Rock Bar ❾ Large, popular disco club offering a choice of commercial house or rock music. ⓐ 1 Wilga Street, Paceville ❶ 2135 3385 ⓦ www.coconut-mt.com ⓔ info@coconut-mt.com

Bugibba & Qawra

Together, Bugibba (pronounced 'Boo-jib-a') and Qawra (pronounced 'Aw-rah') form one of Malta's most important holiday areas. The former consists mainly of apartments, while the latter comprises a handful of large hotels with panoramic views on to Salina Bay. Both resorts have modern, pedestrianised centres with shops, restaurants and bars catering mainly for British tastes.

At Bugibba, a long promenade runs along the waterfront overlooking the lido, offering watersports, cafés and a funfair. Nightlife is lively with numerous late-night bars and discos. Qawra is somewhat quieter, and has good watersports facilities. Amidst all the modern tourist facilities there are two remnants of the era of the Knights.

The **Qawra Tower** at the tip of the peninsula was built by the Grand Master Martin de Redin in the 17th century. At the head of **Salina Bay** is a curious expanse of shallow square depressions cut into the rock. These are saltpans carved out by the Knights in the 17th century and they are still used commercially.

BEACHES & LIDOS

George's Seafront A public beach lido open to all, spread over two levels. On the upper section there is a bar and restaurant, and the lower level has a pool, sundeck and access to the sea. ⓐ Island Promenade, Bugibba

Sunny Coast Popular lido where you can play tennis, use the gym or indoor pool, or simply relax on the sundeck. ⓐ Qawra Road

THINGS TO SEE & DO

Subway Dive Centre
Diving school offering PADI-approved courses for beginners to instructor level. Subway can help to find accommodation nearby if you want to devote your whole visit to diving in Malta.

ⓐ Vista Complex, Pioneer Road, Bugibba ⓣ 2157 2997
ⓦ www.subwayscuba.com

Malta Classic Car Collection
Paradise for lovers of classic cars. The collection was built up over 15 years by the owner, Mr Carol Galea, and is displayed in a museum. A bubble car, Mini Cooper, Corvette and a Thunderbird are among the classics. The museum has a cinema screening films of the golden years of grand prix and classic films featuring automobiles.
ⓐ Tourists Street, Qawra ⓣ 2157 8885 ⓦ www.classiccarsmalta.com
ⓔ info@classiccarsmalta.com

Oracle Casino
Take a chance and make some money at poker or roulette, or throw it away in state-of-the-art slot machines. Dress code is smart casual.
ⓐ Qawra Sea Front ⓣ 2157 0057 ⓦ www.oraclecasino.com
ⓔ win@oraclecasino.com ❶ Entrance fee

AFTER DARK

Restaurants
All Saints £ Situated on the seafront with unobstructed views, this is one of the best places in Qawra for a drink and a pizza. Very popular with locals and visitors. ⓐ Qawra Road ⓣ 2157 3104

Churchill's £ Casual, relaxed dining in attractive surroundings and very reasonably priced. The menu is Maltese and Mediterranean, with a huge choice of pasta, meat and fresh fish of the day. ⓐ Triq il-Fliegu, Qawra ⓣ 2157 2480

Knight's £ Cool kebab house downstairs from Mr Kebab. The décor is modern, the atmosphere informal and you can escape the hustle and bustle. Very reasonably priced and open till late. ⓐ Tourists Street, Bugibba ⓣ 2157 6433

Paderborn £ A cosy restaurant serving Italian and Sicilian-style dishes, pasta and pizza, in a quiet street close to the seafront. ⓐ Gifen Street, Bugibba ⓣ 2158 1205

Incognito ££ A good standard of Maltese and international dishes is on the menu in this highly popular restaurant-pub. Flambés are a speciality. Live music and entertainment nightly. ⓐ Triq Il Fliegu, Qawra ⓣ 2157 2028

Savini £££ Save up for a special night out in an old Maltese farmhouse. The Italian food is anything but fast but this is a place to linger and savour. ⓐ Qawra Road ⓣ 2157 6927

🔺 *Qawra Tower and amazing beach formations*

Nightlife
Bugibba
There are numerous pubs that offer entertainment, pool and karaoke especially. Try The English Bar in St Simon Street, or Paul's Cactus Bar in St Anthony Street.

De Niro's As the name suggests, the bar is themed on the actor Robert De Niro and his images adorn the walls. Serves a wide selection of drinks, cocktails and shooters at very reasonable prices. Party nights hosted by some of the island's top DJs. ⓐ Julio Street, Bugibba ⓣ 2158 1941

Debbie's Galaxy Bar A fun place with quiz nights and karaoke. Good range of beers, local and foreign, wine and spirits. Captain Pawlu organises fishing boat trips on a *luzzu* leaving from the Bugibba jetty at 09.00, returning 15.00. ⓐ 181 St Simon Street, Bugibba ⓣ 2157 4438

Qawra
British-style pubs are clustered in the streets near the bus station.

Amazonia A beach club converted into a series of themed bars and discos. The current 'in' place on the island. ⓐ The Promenade, opposite the Oracle Casino, Qawra ⓣ 2158 1510

Billabong Cocktail Bar A well-stocked bar with a wide selection of cocktails right in the heart of Qawra. Snacks including home-made pastries available. A big-screen TV shows live football, rugby, boxing and the Grand Prix. ⓐ Andrew Cunningham Street, Qawra ⓣ 2157 1470

Fuego Salsa Bar Very popular venue for Latin music and dancing, attracting a broad age range. Located on coast road a short walk from the main promenade of Bugibba and Qawra. DJs play a mix of commercial and pure Latin and keep the party going till dawn. Wednesday night is foam party night. ⓐ Qawra Coast Road, Qawra ⓣ 2138 6746

● *The harbour at St Paul's Bay*

St Paul's Bay

Local tradition has it that St Paul's Bay is the site where the Apostle
Paul was shipwrecked while on his way to trial in Rome in AD 60. He
was washed ashore (together with St Luke) and so brought Christianity
to Malta. Today the little fishing settlement of St Paul's Bay is largely
unaffected by tourism, which has its focus a short distance around the
bay, at Bugibba and Qawra (see pages 24–27).

The harbour, with its bright fishing boats bobbing peacefully in the
water, is one of the most picturesque spots on the island. On the shore
near the town centre is the **Wignacourt Tower**, built by a Grand Master
in 1610, which now houses a small exhibition on Malta's heritage as an
island fortress. ● 09.00–12.00 Mon–Fri.

Out in the bay are two small islands dedicated to St Paul. The larger one boasts a statue. Both can be seen on a boat trip round the bay, which runs from the quay at Bugibba, a short walk away. On the opposite side of the bay to St Paul's is Xemxija (pronounced 'Shem-shee-ya'), meaning sunny place, also with some access to the sea. Beyond is Mistra Bay, a secluded sandy and pebbly inlet. If you want to sunbathe, a much better idea is to visit the lovely sandy beaches of Golden Bay and Ghajn Tuffieha just 6 km (4 miles) east. Beware – they do get very busy in high season and at weekends. Near these beaches are the remains of prehistoric temples, the Roman Baths and the village of Mgarr, with its large church.

BEACHES

The resorts of Bugibba and Qawra are now considered part of St Paul's Bay and are reached easily by the coast road and regular bus routes. There is a small beach at the head of St Paul's Bay itself, but most of the coast in these parts is rocky. Regular buses run to the sandy beaches of Mellieha Bay, 8 km (5 miles) away.

THINGS TO SEE & DO

Horse riding
Very friendly stables at **Golden Bay Horse Riding**, suitable for all standards of rider.
ⓐ Golden Bay (well signposted) ① 2157 3360

Mgarr Church
This handsome baroque church is known as the Egg Church as it was funded largely by the sale of eggs from the village – hence its strange egg-shaped dome (which is best appreciated from a distance).

Mgarr Shelter
Mgarr's World War II underground shelter, opened to the public in 2003, is one of the island's largest; 12m (39 ft) deep and more

than 225m (738 ft) long, it was dug entirely by hand. Oddly, the entrance is through a restaurant.

ⓐ Barri Restaurant, Church Square ⏰ 09.00–14.00 Tues–Sat, 09.00–11.30 Sun ☎ 2157 3235

Roman Baths

The remains of the steam rooms, swimming pool, hot and cold baths and mosaics uncovered at this ancient villa are proof that the pursuit of leisure has a long history on Malta. The ruins are visible through the fence, but for access, the Museums Department requires advance notice.

ⓐ Just over 1.5 km (just under 1 mile) from Ghajn Tuffieha on the road to Mgarr ☎ 2123 9545

Skorba Temples

A Neolithic village was uncovered here, and pottery from the site can be seen in the National Museum of Archaeology in Valletta. The remnants of the two temples are contemporary with Ggantija on Gozo, thought to be the oldest free-standing structures in the world.

ⓐ About 1.5 km (1 mile) east of Mgarr, on the outskirts of Zebbieh ☎ 2158 0590 ⏰ 11.30–13.00 Tues (guided tour)

AFTER DARK

Restaurants

Ciao Bella £ Very pleasant pizzeria with an extensive menu of pizzas and pasta dishes and good value for money. Wide range of fine Maltese wines. ⓐ 5 Mosta Road, St Paul's Bay ☎ 2158 0112 ⏰ 18.30–23.00 Tues–Sun

The Fortress £ Wine bar offering an impressive range of international platters, Maltese, Greek, Chinese and Mexican among them. An outdoor terrace lounge is furnished with white leather armchairs and sofas and has a view across Xemxija Bay. ⓐ Coast Road, Xemxija Bay ☎ 2157 9852 ⓦ www.fortresswineanddine.com

SNAKEBITE
The parish church, **St Paul's Shipwreck**, is said to be built on the spot where the Apostle was bitten by a deadly viper. Apparently unaffected, he threw the snake into the fire beside him, thus enhancing his already saintly reputation.

Nostalgia ££ This is what fine dining is all about. This up-market restaurant specializes in meat dishes – their Chateaubriand is superb. ⓐ 14 Mosta Road ⓣ 2157 5330 ⓛ Reservations recommended

Portobello ££ Located on the hillside overlooking St Paul's Bay and facing westwards, so the sunsets make for a truly romantic evening meal. There are chef's specials every day. The home-made soups are divine. ⓐ St Luke's Street, St Paul's Bay ⓣ 7988 8840

Shaukiwan ££ The best Chinese food in the area, set in a quiet and romantic location, overlooking Xemxija Bay. ⓐ Xemxija Hill ⓣ 2157 3678 ⓛ Daily 19.00–24.00

Zeus ££ A classic Greek restaurant on the main road from St Paul's Bay to Mellieha. ⓐ Xemxija Hill, St Paul's Bay ⓣ 2157 8585

Gillieru £££ One of the area's best restaurants, specialising in fish and seafood and also serving local dishes. Eat inside or on the terrace for wonderful views over the bay. ⓐ 66 Church Street ⓣ 2157 3269/3480 ⓛ 19.30–22.45 ⓘ Reservations recommended

Porto del Sol £££ Fish, seafood and Maltese dishes are the specialities of this up-market restaurant. Superb location with large windows that make the most of the panoramic bay views. Sunday lunch is highly recommended. ⓐ Xemxija Road ⓣ 2157 3970

Mellieha

Mellieha Bay (pronounced 'Mell-ee-ha') is famous for its white sandy beach – easily the longest on the island, at around 600 m (650 yds). It shelves gently into the Mediterranean and is nearly always a colourful sight, with yachts and *luzzus* at anchor, while windsurfers skim the waves. The unspoilt village of Mellieha is perched high above the beach with its landmark parish church looking imperiously down on the seaside activity.

The road sweeps dramatically up from the beach to **Marfa Ridge**, the northernmost part of the island. This is good walking country, although you can also drive to the northern and southern extremities for dramatic sea views. On a clear day, the islands of **Comino** and **Gozo** seem almost within swimming distance, and side roads descend to the lesser-known beaches of **Armier Bay**, **Paradise Bay** and **Ramla Bay**. Ferries depart from Cirkewwa for the island of Gozo (see page 67). On a summer weekend the roads to and from Mellieha are chock-a-block with Maltese beachgoers. If you want to avoid the worst of the crowds, get there early or late – most families will be leaving around 17.00, even though there is a lot of sunshine still left.

BEACHES

Malta's best sandy beaches are in the north, but all are generally quite small and can get crowded. Not far from Mellieha Bay are three superb sandy beaches: **Golden Bay** which is truly beautiful, set in a bay between cliffs; **Gnejna Bay** (pronounced 'Je-nay-na'), a sandy beach with fishermen's boathouses, snack bars and some watersports; and **Ghajn Tuffieha** (pronounced 'Ein-tuff-ee-ha'), a sandy cove in a beautiful natural setting, but the beach is narrow and soon becomes crowded.

Armier Bay This small but attractive sandy beach is used mostly by locals and may provide a less crowded alternative when Mellieha Beach gets too busy – but don't bank on it!

Mellieha Bay (Il Ghadira) Many visitors consider this to be Malta's finest beach. Most watersports are catered for, but the conditions particularly favour windsurfing.

Paradise Bay This lovely sandy cove lies behind the Gozo ferry terminal and is something of a secret to many visitors. On a summer weekend, however, it is packed to the gills with local people.

Ramla Bay This sandy cove is another alternative on the north coast of the Marfa Ridge, though it often catches a swell.

▲ *For a small island, Malta has a lot of fine architecture*

THINGS TO SEE & DO

Adira Sailing Centre & Lido

Sailing school and lido on the outskirts of Mellieha, with RYA-certified instructors. Boards and dinghies available at reasonable rates.
ⓐ Marfa Road, Ghadira Bay ⓣ 2152 3190 ⓦ www.adirasailingcentre. com.mt ⓔ paul.ellul@adirasailingcentre.com.mt

Bird Sanctuary

The Ghadira Bird Sanctuary in Mellieha is one of two wetlands in northern Malta that have been declared Special Areas of Conservation.
ⓣ 2134 7646 or 2134 7667 ⓦ www.birdlifemalta.org
ⓔ info@birdlifemalta.org ⓛ Opening hours vary during the year. Oct–Nov: 10.30–16.30, Dec–Jan: 9.30–15.30, Feb–May: 10.30–16.30

Meldives Diving Centre

Scuba diving for everybody, from complete beginners to advanced divers up to instructor level. PADI and BSAC courses are run every day and the regular programme includes boat, cave, reef and wreck dives.
ⓐ Tunny Net Lido Complex, Marfa Road, Mellieha Bay ⓣ 2152 2595
ⓔ meldives@waldonet.net.mt ⓛ 08.30–16.30 Mon–Sat

Our Lady of the Grotto Chapel

This small, cave-like chapel is one of the oldest places of worship on the island. Local legend has it that St Paul prayed here. Its frescoes date from around the 11th century. The waters of the underground spring are said to have miraculous powers to heal childhood diseases. The steps leading down into the grotto are lined with letters, photos and baby clothes sent by people who have prayed for and received healing.
ⓐ Off Main Street, Mellieha

Project Gaia

The Gaia Foundation is an environmental organisation that manages the protected area of Ghajn Tuffieha Bay. It has a visitor centre and a

small shop selling organic and traditional local products.
🅐 The Elysium Tree Nursery and Visitors' Centre, Ghajn Tuffieha
🅣 2158 4473 🅦 www.projectgaia.org 🅛 08.00–14.30 Tues–Fri,
08.00–13.30 Mon & Sat

Red Tower

Perched on the ridge overlooking Mellieha Bay, the Red Tower was built
in the 17th century to guard the northern coastline and warn the Knights
in Valletta and Mdina of enemy attack.
🅣 9946 07591 🅛 10.00–16.00

Selmun Palace

This handsome 18th-century castle-like palace has been restored and is
now part of a hotel complex, though non-residents may use its high-
class French restaurant. It's worth the detour just to admire its frontage.

Sweethaven Village

Built for the 1980 movie *Popeye*, this film set, resembling a ramshackle
Newfoundland fishing village, continues to pack in the crowds. The village
was built in a photogenic spot, facing a beautiful bay, with a tiny sandy
beach. A small children's amusement park has also sprung up here.
🅣 2157 2430 🅘 Admission charge

AFTER DARK

Restaurants

Armier Lido £ Restaurant, snack bar and pizzeria on spacious terraces,
with a barbecue most evenings after sunset. Great views of Comino and
Gozo. 🅐 Armier Bay, limits of Mellieha 🅣 2157 3539
🅔 armierlido@starwebmalta.com

Crosskeys £ Bar and restaurant serving good-value meat, chicken and
pasta dishes. Also a pizza take-away and karaoke pub. 🅐 Cross Square,
Mellieha 🅣 2152 3744

L'Amigo Bar and Restaurant ££ A good selection of grilled or fried fish, Maltese dishes, chicken, steak, pizza and pasta. Dine upstairs on the open-air veranda. ⓐ 55 G. Borg Olivier Street ⓣ 2152 0822 ⓛ 11.00–14.00, 18.00–22.00, closed Sun

Commando Bar and Restaurant ££ This small restaurant is a good place to try Maltese dishes such as *fenek* (rabbit) or *cerna* (grouper) cooked in wine and herbs. Book a day in advance if you want to try *bragioli* (meat cooked in a traditional stew). ⓐ G. Borg Olivier Street, in the square beside the church ⓣ 2152 3459 ⓛ 09.00–13.30, 19.00–22.00, closed Mon

Giuseppe's ££ Small, intimate and very busy with local people serving local and Italian dishes. ⓐ G. Borg Olivier Street, corner of Triq Santa Liena ⓣ 2157 4882 ⓔ mjdiacono@onvol.net

Ta' Peter ££ The decor is rather bland but the Maltese food is tasty and good value. Book in advance for the three-course Maltese national dish, or choose from fresh fish, meats or a set tourist menu. ⓣ 2152 3537 ⓛ Daily for lunch, dinner and Sun lunch

The Arches £££ One of the island's most up-market restaurants, serving classic continental and Maltese cuisine. Save up and come here on a special occasion. ⓐ G. Borg Olivier Street ⓣ 2152 3460

Le Jardin Restaurant £££ Indulge in langouste (crayfish) 'La Salita', the chef's pride, or fresh fish, grills and meat dishes at this smart restaurant. ⓐ La Salita Antonin Hotel, G. Borg Olivier Street ⓣ 2152 0923

Nightlife
Try **Waves** disco and nightclub, at the beginning of Mellieha Bay beach area. The **Limelight** bar and nightclub in the Mellieha Bay Hotel is open to non-residents.

ⓞ *Malta has many historical remains*

EXCURSIONS

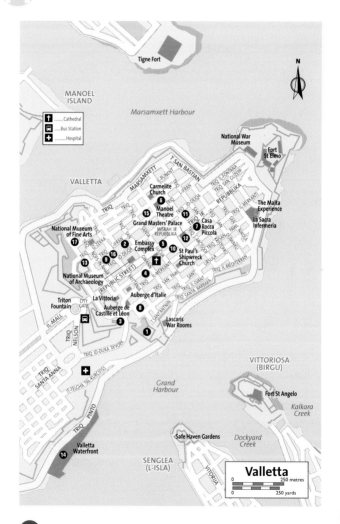

Valletta

Sir Walter Scott called Valletta 'a city built by gentlemen for gentlemen'. The gents in question were the Knights of St John, who built this wonderful city of honey-coloured stone some 430 years ago. Remarkably, it was built in just five years, following the Great Siege of 1565, as the Knights hurried to establish a new fortified capital before the next Turkish onslaught.

Valletta is named after its founder, the Grand Master Jean Parisot de la Vallette. It stretches for nearly 1 km (half a mile) along the hilly peninsula that separates the Grand Harbour and Marsamxett Harbour. The best way to appreciate the grandeur of this great walled city and its enormous bastions is on a harbour cruise (see page 83).

Valletta is easily explored on foot, as it was laid out in a grid pattern. **Republic Street** is the main central thoroughfare, running from Fort St Elmo at the tip of the peninsula to the Triton Fountain by the City Gate. Flights of stone steps worn smooth over the centuries lead up and down the steep and atmospheric side streets of the old town, which are lined with tall limestone houses sporting enclosed balconies, small shops and bars. They open on to grand central squares and shady gardens overlooking the sea.

Five of the eight original *auberges*, the palatial inns that housed the different *langues*, or nationalities, of the Order of St John, have survived. The **Auberge de Castille et Léon**, at Castille Place, has the grandest facade and is now the office of the prime minister. The **Auberge d'Italie** in Merchants Street has been renovated and now houses the Malta Tourism Authority, while the Auberge de Provence houses the **National Museum of Archaeology**. There are a number of churches worth visiting, including **St Paul's Shipwreck Church**, with frescoed ceilings and a relic of the saint; **La Vittoria** (Church of Our Lady of Victories), Valletta's oldest building; and the **Carmelite Church**, its massive dome a prominent landmark.

Valletta has its own rhythms: surging with shoppers and sightseers during the morning and late afternoon, snoozing during the siesta hours. The city is developing a new lease of life at night, with restaurants

> ## THE MALTESE CROSS
> The Maltese Cross became the symbol of the Order of the Knights
> of St John in the mid-13th century. It is white, the colour of purity,
> and its four arms stand for the virtues of Justice, Fortitude,
> Prudence and Temperance. The eight points are given different
> interpretations, a common one is that they represent the
> beatitudes from Christ's Sermon on the Mount.

and wine bars opening in the narrow streets of the city centre and the
Valletta Waterfront development near the cruise-liner terminal.

THINGS TO SEE & DO

Casa Rocca Piccola

This 16th-century palazzo was built for the Italian knight Pietro
La Rocca, and is now the home of his descendant, the 9th Marquis
de Piro, himself a modern-day Knight. Its rooms contain a rich
collection of antique furniture, silver and paintings, and along with
the costume museum give a fascinating insight into the customs
and lifestyle of the Maltese nobility over 400 years.
ⓐ 74 Republic Street ⓣ 2123 1796 ⓛ Guided tours at 10.00, 11.00, 12.00,
13.00 Mon–Sat ❶ Admission charge

Fort St Elmo

An enjoyable guided tour relates the epic story of the Great Siege of 1565
and also gives you a glimpse of the grim former barracks where parts
of the 1978 movie, *Midnight Express*, were filmed.
ⓛ Tours 13.00–17.00 Sat, 09.00–12.00 Sun ❶ Admission charge

Grand Masters' Palace

Built in 1571, this splendid palace was home to the Grand Masters of
the Knights for over 200 years. Today it is the office of the President

of Malta and seat of the country's parliament. The Armouries hold a great collection of military hardware and a lively tour brings the State Apartments to life.

ⓐ Entrance on Merchants Street ☎ 2122 1221 🕒 08.15–17.00 Mon–Sat, 08.15–16.15 Sun (1 Oct–15 June); daily 07.45–14.00 (16 June–30 Sept)
ⓘ Admission charge

Lascaris War Rooms
This warren of underground rooms, within 17th-century tunnels, was the Allied forces' command headquarters during World War II. Operation rooms have been re-created and a headphones tour tells the story of the dark days of 1942 when Malta was under siege.

🔺 *The dining table at Casa Rocca Piccola is laid out in grand style*

🅐 Lascaris Ditch (well signposted along Valletta streets) 📞 2123 4936
🕐 09.30–16.30 Mon–Fri, 09.30–12.30 Sat–Sun

The Malta Experience

This tourist attraction is probably the best of Malta's many audio-visual shows, providing an entertaining general introduction to the island's history and culture.
🅐 Mediterranean Conference Centre, Mediterranean Street
📞 2124 3776 🕐 Show times on the hour, 11.00–16.00 Mon–Fri, 11.00–13.00 Sat & Sun 🅘 Admission charge

Manoel Theatre

Built by the Knights in 1731–2, this ornate theatre with its beautiful gilded ceiling and tiered boxes was restored in 1960 and again in 2003. Attending a performance here is a treat.
🅐 Old Theatre Street 📞 2124 6389 🕐 Tours at 10.30, 11.30 & 16.30 Mon–Fri, 11.30 & 12.30 Sat; theatre season runs Oct–May 🅘 Admission charge

National Museum of Archaeology

Artefacts collected from Malta's many prehistoric temples and burial sites have been gathered here for safekeeping and display. Of special interest are the curious statues of fat women, thought to be fertility symbols.
🅐 Auberge de Provence, Republic Street 📞 2122 1623

National Museum of Fine Arts

The collection of paintings ranges from the early Renaissance to modern times. Of particular interest are works by Mattia Preti, the Italian baroque artist who carried out a lot of the church decoration for the Knights in the 17th century. There is also a collection of artefacts and fine silverware including medical equipment used by the Knights in their hospitals. Later works reflect the changes in governance of Malta, and the highlight of the 19th-century section is a Turner watercolour of the Grand Harbour.
🅐 South Street 📞 2122 5769 ✉ info@heritagemalta.org 🕐 09.00–17.00

SHOPPING

Republic Street is the city's main shopping thoroughfare and there is a daily morning market in Merchants Street. The Sunday Market just outside the City Gate has fallen into the tourist trap with tacky plastic souvenirs, beach towels and T-shirts outnumbering the genuine crafts on sale.

Embassy Complex Malta's first shopping mall and entertainment complex with six floors of retail space, bingo hall, eating places and a six-screen cinema. Cinema 2 has regular presentations of *Malta GC – The Wartime Experience* (stills and archive movie clips telling the story of Malta in World War II). ⓐ St Lucia Street, just off Republic Street ⓣ 2122 7436 ⓦ www.embassycomplex.com.mt ⓛ 09.00–23.00 Mon–Fri, 14.00–23.00 Sat–Sun

The Artisans Centre Has a good selection of quality jewellery, prints and handicrafts. ⓐ 9–10 Freedom Square, near the tourist information office ⓣ 2124 6216 ⓛ 09.00–13.00 & 16.00–19.00 Mon–Fri, 09.00–13.00 Sat

Galea Paintings Artist Aldo Galea's prints and watercolours of Maltese scenes are unique souvenirs of the island. ⓐ 8 Merchants Street ⓣ 2124 3591 ⓛ 09.30–13.00 & 16.00–19.00 Mon–Fri, 09.15–12.45 Sat

The Malta Government Crafts Centre Featuring Maltese handicrafts, with some items for sale. ⓐ St John's Square, opposite St John's Co-Cathedral ⓛ 09.00–13.30 Mon–Fri (16 June–30 Sept); 09.00–12.30 and 15.00–17.00 Mon–Fri (1 Oct–15 June)

The Silversmith's Shop Sells plain and filigree silver jewellery. ⓐ 218 Republic Street ⓣ 2123 1416 ⓛ 09.00–18.00 Mon–Fri, 09.00–13.00 Sat

⬤ *Valletta has grand streets with elegant architecture*

National War Museum

Among the World War II memorabilia on display is the actual George Cross awarded to Malta in 1942 by King George VI, and a restored Gloster Gladiator biplane, Faith, and an Italian E-boat. An annex is devoted to the Royal Navy and the Malta convoys. A vast collection of photographs shows the hardships endured by the civilian population during the bombardment of Malta and the extensive damage caused to Valletta and the surrounding towns by Italian and German bombers in 1942.

ⓐ Fort St Elmo ⊙ 2122 2430 ⊙ 09.00–17.00

La Sacra Infermeria

The 'Holy Infirmary' hospital was built by the Knights in 1574 and reflects their original function as Knights Hospitallers, caring for sick and injured pilgrims in the Middle Ages. It is now occupied by 'The Knights Hospitallers', a series of historical tableaux on the history of the Knights.

ⓐ Mediterranean Street ⊙ 2122 4135 ⊙ 09.00–16.30 Mon–Fri; Knights Hospitallers 09.30–16.00 Sat & Sun ⊙ Admission charge

St John's Co-Cathedral

So-called because it has equal status with the Cathedral in Mdina which is the seat of the Archbishop of Malta and administrative headquarters of the Catholic Church. This magnificent church was built in the 1570s, originally as the main place of worship for the Knights of St John. Grand Masters of the Order are buried in tombs under the marble floor. The Cathedral has eight side chapels, each one dedicated to a *langue*, or nationality, of the noblemen who made up the Knights' fraternity. The chapels have been restored to their former glory with extensive gilding and refurbishment. The Oratory museum holds a Caravaggio masterpiece, *The Beheading of St John*, painted while the young artist was staying in Malta to escape charges of murder in Rome. His *St Jerome* is also on display.

ⓐ St John's Square (entrance on Republic Street) ⊙ 2122 5639
⊙ 09.30–13.00 & 13.30–16.15 Mon–Fri, 09.30–13.00 Sat ⊙ Admission charge. Stiletto-heeled shoes forbidden, and shawls provided for women with bare shoulders.

Saluting Battery, Valletta

Every day at 12.00 a cannon is fired from the old Saluting Battery in Valletta by volunteers from the Malta Heritage Trust dressed in late 19th-century military uniforms. This event re-creates the daily ritual of days gone by. The noon-day gun signalled the exact hour of the day to mariners moored in the harbour. This allowed them to accurately calibrate their ship's timepiece on which they would depend to find the longitude at sea. Guided tours of the historic battery are available on the hour at this site. The location is easily reached on foot from the main bus station following directional signs.

Valletta Waterfront

The Valletta Waterfront is a prestigious new development overlooking the Grand Harbour, with restaurants, cafés and shops set in refurbished old warehouses and workshops. The project is the result of a £15 million investment aimed at regenerating the Grand Harbour quayside into a focal point for entertainment. It stretches about 1 km (half a mile) along Pinto Wharf on the northern shore of the harbour and has quickly become the trendy place to be in the evening in Valletta.

   The Waterfront has won international awards for conservation of the architectural heritage and is a popular venue for arts and music events as well as a popular place to eat or take a stroll. It is the main venue for the annual Malta Jazz Festival in July and a wine fair in August.

TAKING A BREAK

Bars and cafés

Café Barrakka £ ❶   Great for a light al fresco lunch while exploring the sights from Valletta's city fortifications, this café is located just beside the main gate of the Upper Barrakka Gardens. Very reasonably priced snacks, pizzas, Maltese pastries and pasta. The menu has theme nights in the summer (for example, Tuesday is Maltese cuisine, Wednesday and Saturday fresh fish, and Friday is rabbit night with the traditional *fenkata* rabbit in wine stew the star attraction). **ⓐ** Castille Place, Valletta **ⓣ** 2122 3744 **ⓛ** 10.00–16.00 & 19.00–22.00

Chiaroscuro £ **❷** Smart modern coffee bar set in an old building, serving light Italian dishes, baguettes, tortilla wraps and an Italian buffet at lunchtime. In the evening it becomes a wine and cocktail bar, with a wine bar and nightclub in the cellars. The building is over 500 years old and was built as a town house by the Knights; it has also seen service as a monastery and a hotel. **ⓐ** 44 Strait Street, Valletta **ⓣ** 2122 8259 **ⓔ** info@chiaroscuroconcept.com

Inspirations! £ **❸** Coffee shop and a small restaurant within the St James Cavalier Centre for Creativity, an arts centre and exhibition space that is now Malta's national contemporary arts venue. Sandwiches, pastries, fajitas, pizza and salads, served in an open courtyard where artists meet for working lunches and conversation. **ⓐ** Pope Pius V Street, Valletta **ⓣ** 2124 1224 **ⓦ** www.sjcav.org

San Giovanni £ **❹** Just what you need after looking around the Baroque splendours of St John's Co-Cathedral, this outdoor restaurant is immediately outside the Cathedral's exit door. A varied menu of pasta, pizza, fish dishes and some traditional Maltese favourites such as rabbit stew and chicken breast stuffed with ham, cheese and sun-dried tomatoes. **ⓐ** St John Square, Valletta

Caffé Cordina ££ **❺** A city institution. Take a look inside the beautiful interior of the establishment before pulling up a chair on the square outside. **ⓐ** Republic Square **ⓣ** 2123 4385 **ⓛ** 08.30–19.00

Fumia Café ££ **❻** Part of the Manoel Theatre and just the thing for a pre-theatre snack or a coffee break after touring the splendid theatre. Great selection of cakes and pastries. A meeting place for theatre-goers, artists and writers. **ⓐ** Old Theatre Street

AFTER DARK

Restaurants

Bocconi £ ❼ Healthy eating is the thing in Malta's first Italian-style slow-cooking restaurant. Located in the former kitchen of the palace next door, Casa Rocca Piccola. ⓐ 75/76 Republic Street, Valletta ❶ 2123 2505 ⓔ bocconi.malta@gmail.com

La Cave £ ❽ This cosy wine cellar below the Castille Hotel serves pasta, pizza and cheese with wine. ⓐ Castille Square ❶ 2124 3678 ⓛ 12.00–15.00, 18.00–23.00

Cocopazzo £ ❾ A small restaurant that promises a big treat, but that's if you can find it. It's located in an office block in a side street. Specials change every week and the fresh fish includes bream, octopus, snapper and calamari (squid) depending on what the fishermen bring in. ⓐ Valletta Buildings, South Street ❶ 2123 5706

Eddie's Café Regina £ ❿ Enjoy the pizzas, pasta, grilled meats and Maltese dishes at the shady green tables in Republic Square or in the cool, air-conditioned interior. ⓐ Republic Square ❶ 2124 6454 ⓛ 10.00–22.00

Spezzo £ ⓫ A stylish lounge bar and restaurant developed in the building that is home to the Civil Service Sports Club. Mediterranean menu. ⓐ 113 Archbishop Street ❶ 2122 8500 ⓔ spezzo@onvol.net

Blue Room £–££ ⓬ Small, air-conditioned Chinese restaurant with smart blue-and-white décor. Nice variations on the standard dishes, such as spicy seafood and tofu served in earthenware pots. ⓐ Republic Street ❶ 2123 8 014 ⓛ 12.00–15.00, 19.00–23.00 (evenings only Sat, Mon)

Fusion Four ££ ⑬ The place to go for modern-style multicultural dishes that combine local produce with exotic fruit and spices from the Far East, including rabbit-stuffed ravioli and Japanese platters. There is a chic wine bar with a terrace set in the fortifications, located in former stables of the St John cavalry base. ⓐ St John's Cavalier Street, Valletta ① 2122 5255 ⓔ fusion4@maltanet.net

Nan Yuan ££ ⑭ Stylish Chinese restaurant set in the revitalised Valletta Waterfront, with outside tables on the quay. ⓐ Valletta Waterfront ① 2122 5310

Rubino ££ ⑮ The best place in Valletta to experience the range of genuine Maltese cuisine, because the owner, Julian Sammut, is a founder and leading light of the Fulklar Foundation, which aims to celebrate and promote Malta's gastronomic heritage. The menu has all the traditional dishes along with modern creations using only home-grown and fresh-caught ingredients. ⓐ 53 Old Bakery Street, Valletta ① 2122 4656 ⓛ 12.15–14.30 Mon–Fri, 19.45–22.30 Tue–Fri, closed Aug

The Carriage £££ ⑯ Fine cuisine and grand views over the harbour and rooftops of Valletta make this one of the city's best restaurants. The three-course set menu of the week features Mediterranean cooking. ⓐ 22–25 South Street (take the lift from the lobby of Valletta Buildings) ① 2124 7828 ⓛ 12.00–15.30 Mon–Thur, 07.30–23.30 Fri & Sat

Gianinni £££ ⑰ Nouvelle cuisine with an Italian bias, and magnificent views of Marsamxett Harbour. Popular with those with an expense account. Reservations essential. ⓐ 23 Windmill Street ① 2123 7121 ⓛ Mon–Sat (Oct–May) lunch and dinner, closed Sat (June–Sept) lunch

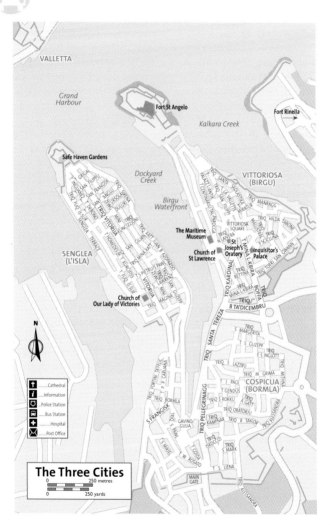

The Three Cities

The Three Cities

The Three Cities – Senglea, Cospicua and Vittoriosa – occupy the finger-like peninsulas jutting into the Grand Harbour from the shore opposite Valletta. They were the first base on Malta for the Knights of St John, who came here in 1530 following their expulsion from Rhodes. Dockyard Creek separates Senglea and Vittoriosa, with Cospicua linking the two on the mainland shores.

The Three Cities are some of the Malta's most historic towns, but, because they lack major hotels, restaurants and tourist facilities, visitors generally overlook them. A harbour cruise gives a tantalising glimpse of the handsome waterfront buildings, and of the old-fashioned *dghajsas* (pronounced 'day-sas') – Malta's version of gondolas – drifting peacefully in Senglea's harbour. Anyone who returns to explore the Three Cities in more detail will be rewarded with a taste of Malta as it was in the days before mass tourism.

The Knights first established themselves at Birgu because it provided shelter for their ships. They set about fortifying the dilapidated Fort St Angelo at the tip and constructing their first *auberges* and palaces. By the 1560s the growing city had spread beyond the walls to form the suburb of Bormla, now known as Cospicua. Meanwhile, the separate town of L'Isla, renamed Senglea after the French Grand Master Claude de la Sengle following the construction of Fort St Michael in 1552, arose on the opposite peninsula. Birgu was renamed Vittoriosa in honour of the Knights' victory over the Turks in the Great Siege of 1565, though many locals still call it by its original name. When the new capital of Valletta was built, the fortunes of the Three Cities began to decline. However, lines of defences continued to be built around them well into the 17th century.

With the development of the shipbuilding and shipping industries at nearby Marsa, dockyard workers made their homes in the Three Cities. But they also became targets for bombing raids during World War II, with Senglea and Cospicua suffering extensive damage.

THINGS TO SEE & DO

VITTORIOSA

Vittoriosa has a fine old town centre and is the most atmospheric of
the Three Cities. A stroll along its narrow, winding streets reveals many
delights, such as the lovely architecture of Victory Square, which is
surrounded by the *auberges* of England, Germany and Auvergne et
Provence. The three elegant gateways at the landward side of the city –
Advanced Gate, Couvre Porte and Provence Gate – were built in the early
18th century. The Post of England lookout on the Kalkara Creek side has
views of the former Bighi Naval Hospital and the old Ricasoli Fort on
adjacent peninsulas.

Church of St Lawrence

This landmark of Vittoriosa's waterfront, with its dome and twin
clock towers, is a 17th-century reconstruction of the Knights'
original Conventual Church. The interior is richly decorated
with red marble, frescoes and an outstanding painting,
The Martyrdom of St Lawrence by Mattia Preti. In front of the church,
the Freedom Monument commemorates the British withdrawal
from Malta in 1979.

ⓐ St Lawrence Street ⊕ 2182 7057 ⓒ 09.30–12.00, 16.30–17.30

Fort St Angelo

The Knights fortified an earlier castle on this strategic point and from
here they repelled the Turks during the Great Siege. The first Grand
Masters and many Knights are buried here. It later became a prison and
was a naval base for the Allies during World War II.

ⓐ Guided tours every 15 minutes, 09.00–13.00 Sat (June–Sept);
10.00–14.00 (Oct–May) ❶ Admission charge

The Inquisitors' Palace

Built in 1574, this palace was the headquarters of the Inquisition in
Malta. Gruesome tortures took place here, as the hated Inquisitors

> **THE GREAT CHAIN**
> The Knights had a secret weapon for defending the Three Cities
> during the Great Siege. An enormous chain, which had been
> forged in Venice, was strung across the entrance to Dockyard Creek
> between Senglea and Fort St Angelo. A remnant can still be seen
> below the fort.

sought to extract 'confessions' of heresy. The museum contains furniture
and household goods. You can also visit the courtroom, main hall, chapel
and dungeons, where the prisoners' graffiti are still visible.
🄰 Main Gate Street 🕿 2182 7006 🕐 09.00–17.00 ❗ Admission charge

The Maritime Museum
Malta's naval history is illustrated with photos, models of the galleys
of the Knights and of traditional Maltese fishing vessels, and even
medieval navigation tools.
🄰 Dockyard Creek 🕿 2166 0052 🕐 09.00–17.00 ❗ Admission charge

St Joseph's Oratory
Built as a chapel behind the church of St Lawrence in the 18th century,
the oratory is now a small museum containing artefacts brought by the
Knights from Rhodes. Grand Master Jean de la Vallette's hat and sword,
and a crucifix used at executions, are here.
🄰 Vittoriosa Square 🕐 09.30–12.00, 14.00–16.00 Mon–Sat,
09.30–12.00 Sun

COSPICUA
Like neighbouring Senglea, Cospicua was heavily bombed during
World War II and there is little to see in its narrow, stepped streets.
The ornate Church of the Immaculate Conception, built in 1637, is one
of the few buildings to have escaped destruction and is worth a look.
The city is enclosed by a double ring of bastions, the landward

defences built by the Knights. The inner Margherita Lines, with six bastions, were begun in 1639. Between 1670 and 1680, the Cotonera Lines, funded by Grand Master Nicolas Cotoner, were built beyond. The Zabbar Gate is the best of the finely carved triumphal gateways that break the curtain walls.

Fort Rinella

Fort Rinella, built by the British in the 19th century, lies north-east of the Three Cities. It contains the world's largest cannon, the Armstrong 100 ton. Historical re-enactments take place daily during the summer at 14.30. Guided tours on the hour include the firing of a period gun.
ⓐ St Rocco Road, Kalkara (bus 4 from Valletta) ☎ 2180 0992
🕙 10.00–17.00 ❶ Admission charge

SENGLEA

Senglea was heavily bombed during World War II. Victory Street, the main thoroughfare, runs from the main square to the gardens on the peninsula. There is also an attractive waterfront along Dockyard Creek.

Church of Our Lady of Victories

The church, in the main town square, was badly damaged in the bombing but is now restored to its former glory, with a fine, painted dome.

Safe Haven Gardens

Also called Gardjola Garden, these gardens surround the picturesque Vedette, or lookout post, on the tip of the peninsula and offer superb panoramic views of the entire Grand Harbour. The *vedette* is a six-sided

> ### MALTA AT WAR MUSEUM
> Small museum dedicated to the civilian struggle during World War II. The main attraction is a guided tour of the underground air-raid shelter. ⓐ Courve Porte Gate, Vittoriosa ☎ 2189 6617
> 🕙 10.00–16.00 ❶ Admission charge

tower, finely carved with two eyes and two ears to signify vigilance against enemy ships. It is one of the few survivors of pre-World War II Senglea. The gardens were created on the site of Fort St Michael, which was built by the Knights and dismantled by the British to create docks for the Royal Navy.

🔺 *Vittoriosa's waterfront landmark, the Church of St Lawrence*

Medieval Mdina

Malta's old capital is the island's most perfectly preserved medieval town. It is a world away from noisy modern-day resort life and even the gentle bustle of Valletta is a comparative cacophony. Here in the quiet narrow streets and alleyways, you can almost touch the sense of history.

The Romans were the first to settle in this area, attracted, like their successors, by its strategic situation: high inland, easy to defend and surrounded by fertile agricultural countryside. But if the name Mdina (pronounced 'Im-deena') sounds Arabic then that is not surprising. It derives from the word *medina*, meaning 'the City' and was so named by the Arabs who conquered Malta in 870 and stayed for two centuries, making the city their stronghold and capital.

Sadly, there is virtually nothing left from this period and it was left to the Knights of St John to give Mdina its current form. They fortified the city, made it their cavalry headquarters and called it Citta Notabile, meaning 'The Eminent City'. The Knights did not stay long, however. After the Great Siege of 1565 they moved to Valletta and so the demise of Mdina began. It became known as the 'Old City' and, as it began to fade away quietly, was renamed the 'Silent City'.

Thanks to tourism, Mdina is no longer silent, by day at any rate. Restaurants, shops and a handful of attractions draw visitors, and residents' own motor vehicles disturb the slumber (though no other vehicles are allowed in). At night, however, the city's 400 or so inhabitants enjoy what must be the quietest sleep in all Malta. A visit after dark, when the empty, dimly lit streets fall totally silent, is highly recommended.

The entrance to the city is through the splendid Main Gate, built in 1724, which lies across a bridge spanning the dry moat. The three statues on the inside facade are St Publius, St Paul and St Agatha, Malta's three patron saints. Nearly all of Mdina's sightseeing interest lies along the main street, Triq Villegaignon. Walk slowly and gaze upwards to admire the facades of the various *palazzi* (mansions) along here. The most eminent address is the Casa Inguanez, the home of Malta's oldest aristocratic family.

⬥ *Main Gate, Mdina*

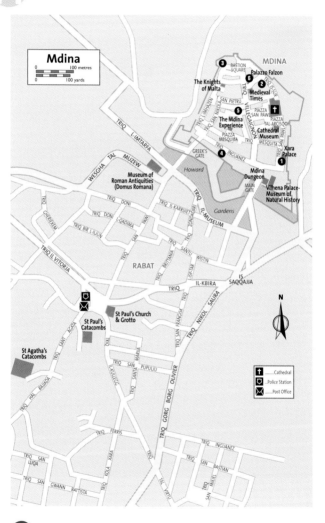

THINGS TO SEE & DO

Bastion Square

At the end of Triq Villegaignon, Bastion Square makes the perfect end to a stroll through Mdina. From the city walls there are sweeping views across the plains below. Even on the dullest day the giant dome of Mosta's church is a mighty landmark and you should be able to see all the way to Valletta and almost right along both coasts to St Paul's Bay in the north and to Marsascala in the south.

Cathedral

Built in 1697–1702 by Lorenzo Gafa after the earlier church was destroyed by an earthquake, St Paul's Cathedral is second only to St John's Co-Cathedral in Valletta in grandeur. The rich baroque interior is one of the finest on Malta; the vaulted ceiling is adorned with frescoes by Mattia Preti while colourful funerary slabs cover the floor. Other highlights include the high altar of marble and lapis lazuli, and a Byzantine icon of the Madonna and Child in a side chapel.
ⓐ St Paul's Square ⓣ 2145 4136 ⓛ 09.30–16.30 Mon–Sat, 15.00–16.30 Sun
ⓘ Admission charge combined with ticket to Cathedral Museum

Cathedral Museum

Housed in an 18th-century baroque palace, this museum features numerous works of art, some by famous Old Masters. The highlight is the collection of woodcuts by Albrecht Dürer depicting the Small Passion of Christ and the Life of the Virgin.
ⓐ St Paul's Square ⓣ 2145 4697 ⓛ 09.30–16.30 Mon–Fri, 09.30–15.00 Sat
ⓘ Admission charge includes visit to Cathedral

The Knights of Malta

Located in historic gunpowder vaults, these tableaux depict the life and times of the Knights with appropriate sound effects.
ⓐ 14–19 Magazine Street ⓣ 2145 1342 ⓛ 10.00–17.00 Mon–Sat, 10.00–16.00 Sun ⓘ Admission charge

Mdina Dungeon

Some of the scenes in here may look like pure dark fantasy, but these are real dungeons and what you see is an exhibition of real medieval Maltese horror – everything portrayed here actually happened (though not necessarily in these dungeons). If you are squeamish or you have young children in tow, give it a miss.

ⓐ St Publius Square, just inside the Main Gate ⓣ 2145 0267
ⓛ 09.30–16.00 ❶ Admission charge

The Mdina Experience

This audio-visual show in a comfortable air-conditioned auditorium gives a good general introduction to the history of the city. There is a café on site.

ⓐ 7 Mesquita Square ⓣ 2145 4 322 ⓛ 09.30–16.30 Mon–Sat, 09.30–15.30 Sun ❶ Admission charge

Medieval Times

Compared with the dungeons, this is a rather humdrum series of tableaux depicting medieval life in Malta.

ⓐ In the Palazzo Notabile, Triq Villegaignon ⓣ 2145 4625
ⓛ 09.00–17.00 ❶ Admission charge

Museum of Natural History

The handsome 18th-century Vilhena Palace is home to Mdina's old-fashioned natural history museum. It is as dry in tone as some of the bones it displays, but worth a visit.

ⓐ St Publius Square, adjacent to the Mdina Dungeon ⓣ 2145 5951
ⓛ 09.30–16.30 ❶ Admission charge

Palazzo Falzon

Also known as the Norman House; this 14th-century mansion contains a small museum of naval art and antique furniture.

ⓐ Triq Villegaignon ⓣ 2145 4512 ⓛ 10.00–17.00 Tues–Fri, 08.00–19.00 Sat & Sun ❶ Admission charge (includes audio guide)

TAKING A BREAK

AD 1530 £ ❶ Bright trattoria serving pizza, pasta, salads and light snacks. ⓐ Adjacent to the Xara Palace Hotel ☎ 2145 0560

Fontanella £ ❷ Famous for home-made cakes and the view along the ramparts near Bastion Square. Sandwiches and salads are also available. ⓐ 1 Bastion Street ☎ 2145 4264 🕐 10.00–22.00 (summer); 10.00–18.00 (winter)

AFTER DARK

Restaurants
Ciappetti £ ❸ Charming courtyard restaurant serving Italian specialities, with a terrace upstairs on the bastion. ⓐ 5 St Agatha's Esplanade ☎ 2145 9987 🕐 11.00–15.30, 19.30–23.00

Bacchus ££ ❹ Two chambers of a 17th-century gunpowder magazine in a fortified bastion of the town walls make a unique setting for one of Mdina's best restaurants. Speciality fish dishes, grills, pasta, soups and salads are on the menu. ⓐ Inguanez Street ☎ 2145 4981 🕐 09.00–21.00

Medina ££ ❺ Located in a house dating back to the 11th century, the best tables are in an inner courtyard covered with vines. The interior has vaulted stone ceilings and in winter there are roaring wood fires. The menu is varied French, Mediterranean and Maltese, and there is a vegetarian selection. ⓐ 7 Holy Cross Street, Mdina ☎ 2145 4004 ⓔ info@medinarestaurant.com 🕐 19.00–23.00 Mon–Sat

Palazzo Notabile ££ ❻ Coffee shop and restaurant in a beautiful setting in a 17th-century baroque palace. Mediterranean and Italian cuisine including Maltese dishes. ⓐ Triq Villegaignon ☎ 2145 4625 🕐 10.00–16.00, 19.00–22.30 Mon–Sat, 10.00–16.00 Sun

Rabat

Rabat, meaning 'the suburb' in Arabic, lies just outside Mdina's city walls. The two were one city in Roman times, and became separated when the Arabs began building smaller fortifications around Mdina. Rabat has always acted as the commercial quarter for the old capital and continues to be a lively market town with plenty of historical interest.

Rabat is a sprawling town with some 13,000 residents, a commercial hub for much of central Malta. Its main sights, however, are all located around the central Parish Square, about a ten-minute walk from Mdina's historic main gate. There is a colourful fruit and vegetable market in the square on weekdays. Few concessions to tourism impinge on the traditional local character of Rabat, and its streets are lined with lovely old-style houses with ornate, enclosed balconies. A multitude of saints' statues atop their wooden plinths lines the streets during the annual summer *festa* (town festival).

Rabat is most famous for its early Christian **catacombs** (underground tunnels with niches for tombs). Below the streets lies a labyrinth of these underground tunnels, covering more than 2.5 square km (a square mile) in area. Malta's catacombs, unlike those in Rome, were not hiding places for persecuted Christians. They were used solely as burial chambers, and pagans and Jews were also interred here. There are various types of tombs: floor graves; canopy tombs; and small graves, known as *loculi*, cut into the wall to hold the body of a child.

The most unusual feature of the catacombs is the circular agape tables, which were carved out of the rock so that relatives of the dead could gather underground for ritual funeral and anniversary feasts with their departed loved ones. Two sets of catacombs are open to the public.

🔺 *St Paul's Church, Rabat*

THINGS TO SEE & DO

Domus Romana

Apart from the mosaic floor, little is left of the old Roman villa, but the museum built on site contains a collection of *amphorae* (ancient Roman jars), glass, oil lamps, olive crushers and other artefacts.

ⓐ Museum Esplanade ⓣ 2145 4125 ⓛ 09.00–17.00 ⓘ Admission charge

St Agatha's Catacombs

These catacombs, dedicated to the Sicilian martyr St Agatha, are outstanding for their late Roman and medieval frescoes, dating from the 3rd to 5th centuries. A guide points out the highlights on a tour lasting 20–30 minutes. You can browse through the convent's small museum, with an eclectic collection of minerals, pottery, ancient statuettes and other artefacts.

ⓐ St Agatha Street ⓣ 2145 4503 ⓛ 09.00–17.00 ⓘ Admission charge

St Paul's Catacombs

Malta's largest catacombs once contained some 1,400 graves. You can wander through the eerie maze of lighted passages on your own, starting from a simple chapel near the entrance.

ⓐ St Agatha Street ⓣ 2145 4562 ⓛ 09.00–17.00
ⓘ Admission charge

St Paul's Church and Grotto

Rabat's parish church dates from the 16th century. The Grotto of St Paul lies beneath the adjoining Chapel of St Publius and is reached by a separate entrance. According to local tradition, St Paul took shelter here for several months following his shipwreck on Malta while he preached Christianity to the islanders. The grotto walls supposedly have healing powers. Behind the large marble statue of the saint is a series of catacombs.

ⓐ Parish Square ⓣ 2145 4467 ⓛ 09.00–16.00 Mon–Sat ⓘ Donation

AFTER DARK

Restaurants

Jerry's Chopsticks £ A relaxed and unpretentious Chinese restaurant in Rabat just outside the gate to Mdina, serving classic dishes with a twist, such as whole fish with pineapple sauce. ⓐ Saqqajja Square ⓣ 2145 6789

The Roadhouse Buskett £ A great place to bring children. The restaurant is set in Malta's only forest, Buskett Gardens, and on Sundays provides children's entertainment with a bouncy castle and other park toys. At night the outside area serves as a nightclub. ⓐ Buskett Gardens, outskirts of Rabat ⓣ 2145 4233

Roman's Den £ Rustic cosy basement bar and dining room on the main road through Rabat, where on Friday nights there are cheap drinks and a DJ playing R&B, soul and hip-hop. ⓐ Main Street ⓣ 2145 6970

La Veduta £ The restaurant is perched on top of the hill outside the walls of Mdina and has a stunning view over central Malta out to sea. Serving good value plain food, grills, chicken, pizzas and salads, La Veduta is popular among Maltese families. ⓐ Saqqajja Square ⓣ 2145 4666

Il-Palazz l-Ahmar ££ A delightful family-run restaurant in a 16th-century country lodge on the outskirts of Rabat towards Mtahleb. Owners Tony and Annette Grech are well known for their hospitality and fabulous Maltese food. ⓐ Wied il-Busbies, Landrijiet ⓣ 2145 2003

Ristorante Cosmana Navarra ££ Dishes range from *confit* of duck, rabbit stew and fish in the upstairs restaurant, to snacks in the downstairs bar. ⓐ 28 St Paul's Street, situated opposite the church ⓣ 2145 0638 ⓛ 18.30–22.00 Mon–Sat; bar open daily until midnight

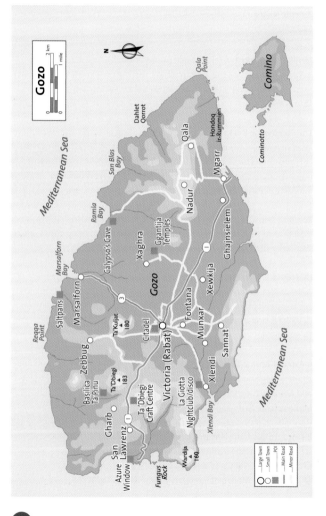

Gozo

Legend has it that Gozo is the legendary island of Calypso, the sea nymph who, in Homer's *Odyssey*, kept Odysseus captive for seven years. You may not stay that long, but you will most certainly feel the ancient attraction of the island's temples, standing stones and time-worn landscapes.

Many visitors wrongly assume that Gozo is just an extension of its larger sister, Malta. Though its villages are built from the same honey-coloured limestone, Gozo has a completely different feel. Guest accommodation is primarily in holiday apartments, farmhouses and upmarket hotels rather than in large resorts, so the atmosphere is quieter and the pace is slower. Gozo is Malta's market garden, and the landscape here is noticeably greener, especially in the sun-baked summer. The hillsides and valleys are covered with fertile orchards and terraced fields that are still worked using traditional methods. On the north coast, near **Reqqa Point**, people harvest sea salt from the saltpans as their ancestors have done for centuries.

Gozo's capital, **Victoria**, lies roughly in the centre of the island and a visit to its historic citadel is a must. The hilltop towns of **Nadur**, **Xaghra** (pronounced 'Shah-ruh') and **Zebbug**, with their prominent church domes, are known as the 'three hills' and they are the island's original settlements. The fishing villages of **Marsalforn** and **Xlendi** (pronounced 'Shlen-di'), set around attractive bays, have developed as the main resorts for tourists.

Diving and swimming are excellent in the clear blue waters around Gozo's coastline. There are also good walks, both along the coast and inland. Although the island is small – only 64 sq km (26 sq miles) – there are enough places of interest to keep you busy for a fortnight. However, Gozo is not meant for rushing around, but for relaxing on its idyllic bays, sipping a coffee or a beer at its local bars and cafés, or enjoying a meal at its pleasant restaurants.

The ferry crossing from Cirkewwa on Malta to Mgarr on Gozo takes about 25 minutes. In high season the morning ferry gets very busy, so get there early.

BEACHES

Dahlet Qorrot Set around a little harbour backed by colourful fishermen's huts, this small sandy beach is popular with local families. There is also a very good coastal walk from here to Qala Point.

Hondoq ir-Rummien This small sandy beach below the village of Qala faces the island of Comino. It is good for children but can get very crowded at weekends.

Ramla Bay This wide stretch of soft reddish sand is Gozo's best beach, but, thankfully, it remains surprisingly uncrowded. Approach it on the road from Marsalforn. Above the beach is the fabled Calypso's Cave, now reduced by rock falls to a mere cleft in the rock, but a vantage point for a picture-postcard view.

San Blas This is the best little sandy cove in Gozo. It's quite a trek getting down to it and an even longer one climbing back up, but if you're fit and child-free, the good swimming here makes the effort well worthwhile.

THINGS TO SEE & DO

Ager Foundation

A new organisation to promote the culture, nature, history and typical traditions of Gozo. They offer walking tours and workshops on conservation and traditional rural practices, such as cheese-making and sheep-shearing.

ⓣ 2156 4378 ⓦ www.agerfoundation.com ⓔ ager.foundation@gmail.com

The Azure Window

Eroded limestone has never been so spectacular as at Gozo's aptly named Azure Window at Dwejra Bay. Behind it, reached by a tunnel, is the saltwater lake known as the Inland Sea. If you can watch the

◆ *Victoria Square, Xaghra, with its parish church*

sunset from here it will be a highlight of your holiday. Nearby is the offshore outcrop known as Fungus Rock, so-called because of a spongy plant, *fungus melitensis*, that grew there. It was used to cure stomach pains and to stem the flow of blood from injuries, and was so prized by the Knights that they built Qawra Tower opposite to guard the supply.

Calypso's Cave
According to legend this is where the nymph Calypso kept Odysseus a 'prisoner of love' for seven years. More practically, this is a spot high on the cliffs from where you get a stunning view of the shoreline and Ramla Bay, famous for its beach of red sand. The viewpoint is easily reached by road and there is a winding footpath down to the beach.

Diving

Gozo is noted for dramatic underwater rock formations, caves and tunnels and is excellent for diving. There are numerous dive centres. **St Andrew's Diving Cove** is a fully equipped and PADI-certified dive centre open all year and caters for first-timers and divers looking for

◯ *Gozo's capital, Victoria, has interesting backstreets*

certification. ⓐ St Simon Street, Xlendi Bay, Gozo ❶ 2155 1301
ⓦ www.gozodive.com
Altantis Diving Centre is in Marsalforn and offers PADI-certified courses
and excursions. ⓐ Qolla Street, Marsalforn, Gozo
❶ 2155 4685 ⓦ http://atlantisgozo.com ⓔ diving@atlantisgozo.com
Frankie's Gozo Dive Centre offers beginners' dives, PADI courses and
diving holidays on their motor sailing yacht. ⓐ Mgaar Road, Xewkija,
Gozo ❶ 2155 1315 ⓦ www.gozodiving.com ⓔ info@gozodiving.com

Ggantija

Along with Malta's other ancient temples, these 5,000-year-old remains
are the Earth's oldest free-standing structures, pre-dating even the
pyramids and Stonehenge.
ⓐ Located on the outskirts of Xaghra
❶ 2155 3194 ❷ 09.00–17.00 Mon–Sat ❶ Admission charge

Gharb Folklore Museum

All kinds of interesting commercial and domestic bygones are displayed
in a beautifully restored 18th-century house. Definitely worth a visit.
ⓐ 99 Church Square, Gharb ❶ 2156 1929 ❷ 09.30–16.00 Mon–Sat,
09.30–12.00 Sun ❶ Admission charge

Gozo Jeep Tours

A great way to get around the island and see all the beauty spots in a
day, with an expert guide. To drive a jeep you must be over 25 years old
and have a valid driving licence.
ⓐ 45 St Lucy Street, St Lucia, Kercem, Gozo ❶ 2156 1817

Marsalforn

Gozo's largest resort sits in a wide bay with its colourful fleet of
traditional *luzzus* (pronounced 'lut–sues') sheltered in a tiny harbour
next to the small sandy beach. There are good waterfront restaurants
and bars, a promenade, watersports and bicycle hire. The saltpans
along the shore to the west of the village are a unique sight.

Victoria

The island's tiny capital was named in honour of Queen Victoria's diamond jubilee in 1897 (locals still use the old name, Rabat). Independence Square is a charming spot with trim shady trees, old-fashioned shops, a handful of cafés and a morning market. Just off the square, the 17th-century Church of St George is known as the 'Golden Basilica' on account of its rich gilded baroque interior. The medieval lanes behind the square are fun to explore.

The walled citadel perched above the streets of Victoria dates back to Roman times and was fortified by the Knights of St John in the early 17th century. The panoramic views over the island from the ramparts are stupendous. Behind its rather plain façade, the cathedral is a baroque gem with a most unusual feature: when the funds ran out to complete the planned dome, the Italian artist, Antonio Manuele, painted a *trompe-l'oeil* dome. It was probably the only parish church on Gozo for several centuries.

Housed within the citadel precincts are several small museums, the best of which is the **Folklore Museum**, but there's also the **Old Prison**, **Natural Science Museum**, **Museum of Archaeology and Cathedral Museum**. ❶ 2155 6087 (Cathedral), 2155 3194 (Heritage Malta for all museums) ❷ 09.00–17.00 (Cathedral Museum closed Sun)

TAKING A BREAK

Bellusa Café £ Small friendly café in an old town house near the fish market. The tables outside are ideal for people-watching in Victoria's main square. ⓐ 34 Independence Square, Victoria ❶ 2155 6243 ❷ 07.00–19.00

Brookies Pub & Restaurant ££ Family-run restaurant situated beneath the walls of the citadel. The fish is very good. Pasta and local dishes are also on the menu. ⓐ 1–2 Wied Sara Street, Victoria, on the main road to Zebbug ❶ 2155 9524 ❷ Lunch and dinner, closed Tues

Otters Bistro ££ Stylish modern eatery on the water's edge with a terrific view of Marsalforn Bay. Excellent salads, pasta and fish, and great wine selection. ⓐ Saint Mary Road, Marsalforn ⓣ 2156 2473 ⓛ 10.00–01.00 (summer); 10.00–15.00 and 19.00–24.00 (winter)

AFTER DARK

Restaurants
Ta'Rikardu (Riccardo's) £ Cosy family-owned restaurant in the narrow lanes of the Citadel in Victoria close to the Cathedral. The fresh home-made vegetable soup is fabulous but never the same from one day to the next. Gozitan salad of peppered goat's cheese, tomatoes, onion, capers and olives is a speciality. Also unusual is rabbit in orange sauce, not seen in Malta. A small shop sells Gozitan produce, honey, liqueurs and hand-crafted glass. ⓐ 4 Triq il-Fosos, Cittadella, Victoria ⓣ 2155 5953

Xerri Il-Bukkett £ Gorgeous views over Mgarr harbour to Comino and Malta are to be had from the terrace of this hilltop bar and restaurant. The local *bocci* (a game like *boules*) club is adjacent to the bar. ⓐ Zewwieqa Road, Qala ⓣ 2155 3500 ⓛ Daily

L'Ankra ££ You can watch the boats coming and going from the big windows of this restaurant overlooking Mgarr harbour. Fresh fish, pasta and local specialities. ⓐ 11 Shore Street, Mgarr ⓣ 2155 5656 ⓛ Lunch and dinner

Chez Amand ££ This delightful bistro and restaurant, with a cool terrace overlooking the beach, serves delicious Maltese specialities and Mediterranean dishes, such as *gbejniet* (cheese) salad, seafood *amandine* and *canneloni thermidor*. A friendly spot run by Belgian chef Amand and his daughter Caroline. ⓐ Qbajjar Bay, Marsalforn ⓣ 2156 1188 ⓛ Closed Wed (July–Sept); dinner only on Fri and Sat (Nov–Mar)

Huan Yuan ££ Highly rated Cantonese restaurant on the hill leading up from Mgarr Harbour, next to L'Ankra. ⓐ Shore Street, Mgarr ⓣ 2156 5700 ⓛ 18.30–23.00 daily, 12.00–14.30 Sun lunch

Il-Kartell ££ Set in three adjacent former boathouses in the harbour of Marsalforn with a summer terrace on the water's edge. Varied menu of Mediterranean and Maltese dishes, including plain grilled fresh fish and *qara baghli mimli* – marrow stuffed with minced pork, beef and cheese. ⓐ Marina Street, Marsalforn ⓣ 2155 6918 ⓛ 11.30–15.30 and 18.00–22.30

Salvina ££ A beautifully restored rustic house serving excellent island dishes. ⓐ 21 Triq Frenc ta'l-Gharb ⓣ 2155 2505 ⓛ 12.00–15.00 and 18.00–22.00; dinner only in summer, closed Thur all day

SHOPPING

Handmade lace is a Gozitan speciality and highly prized for its quality. Best deals are in the craft shops at **Ta'Dbiegi Crafts Village**, located in a former army barracks in St Lawrenz. Rosanna's, located at Shop 2, has a vast array of lace, hand-knitted woollens, shawls, tablecloths and other items at very reasonable prices. **Pins & Needles** produces hand-crafted leather items on site, including passport covers, purses, key fobs and belts. **Ta'Dbiegi Jewellery** in Workshop 1 is a small workshop where you can see a range of gold and silver items being made.

Look for **Gbejniet**, Gozo's tasty sheep's milk cheese, which you can buy as small peppery rounds in jars from the market in Victoria, or from shops.

Arkadia is Victoria's shopping mall in Fortunato Mizzi Street, and has some interesting boutiques. **Junction 66** has high-quality gifts, fine glassware, china figurines and wooden clocks.

Stone Crab ££ Some of the best fish on Gozo can be had at this water-side restaurant. Carnivores can tuck into an excellent steak rossini.
ⓐ Xlendi Bay ⓣ 2155 9315 ⓦ www.thestonecrab.com ⓛ Lunch and dinner (Apr–Oct); Sat and Sun only (Nov and Feb–Mar), closed Dec–Jan

Nightlife
La Grotta is a popular disco club in the countryside near the fishing village of Xlendi. It's partly in a cave with an open-air dance floor.
ⓐ Xlendi Road, Munxar (about 2 km/1 mile) from Victoria) ⓣ 2155 1149
ⓛ 23.00–early morning (summer only)

Victoria has two opera houses, the Aurora and the Astra, built by rival philharmonic societies and still going strong. When there is no opera, the theatres are used as cinemas.

● *The island's buses are colourful period pieces*

Comino

Midway between Malta and Gozo, and covering just 2.5 sq km (1 sq mile), Comino is the smallest of Malta's inhabited islands. It takes its name from the herb, cumin, which grew wild here in former times. Once a pirate haven, the island is now home to an away-from-it-all hotel specialising in watersports, plus a handful of farmers who somehow eke a living from this barren, sun-baked rock. There are no roads and no cars. Some tours allow you to explore the island, though there is little to see, apart from the hotel, an ancient chapel and the Santa Marija watchtower (which doubled as the Chateau d'If in the 2002 movie *The Count of Monte Cristo*), built by the Knights in the early 17th century. Surprisingly, this tiny spot has a police station, and Mass is held once a week in the old chapel.

Comino's great attraction is the Blue Lagoon. Its heavenly turquoise waters above a seabed of soft white sand are fantastic for swimming and snorkelling, and the underwater caves and grottoes are perfect for scuba divers. However, the tiny cove can become very crowded with day-trippers and cruise-boat passengers. If you want to swim, stick to the lagoon as there are jellyfish in the harbour and their stings can be quite painful. On the opposite shore is the uninhabited rock islet of Cominotto.

Most people visit Comino as part of a day cruise from Malta or Gozo. In summer there are also small boats that ferry passengers on the 15-minute trip to the Blue Lagoon from Cirkewwa harbour several times a day; from Gozo the ten-minute ferry trip operates on a regular basis. If you decide to explore Comino, take plenty of water, a hat and extra sun cream, as there is little shade. The hotel is closed in winter, so bring food and drink as well if you visit then.

◀ *Comino's fabulous Blue Lagoon*

Malta panorama

The centre of the island holds much of interest, and a day away from the resorts will do much to round out your experience of Malta. The easiest way to do this is to take a tourist coach tour. The itinerary can vary, but typically begins at one of Malta's most remarkable churches at Mosta, travels back in time to the island's original capital at Mdina, visits the Ta'Qali crafts village for a bit of shopping, stops for lunch at a village restaurant and ends at the picture-postcard fishing village of Marsaxlokk. If you hire a car, there are also temples and gardens to explore.

THINGS TO SEE & DO

Marsaxlokk

The name Marsaxlokk (pronounced 'Marsa-shlock') derives from *marsa* (the port) and *xlokk* (the sirocco wind). This is the most picturesque fishing village in Malta and, despite the coach-loads of visitors it receives daily, it has remained remarkably unspoiled. Its quayside is the perfect place for a cheap fish lunch and there is a daily market where you can haggle over lace tablecloths and other goods.

Limestone Heritage

An unusual tourist attraction giving an insight into Malta's traditional stoneworking, located in an old quarry from which the rich honey-coloured limestone was extracted. You can try your hand at chiselling a piece of limestone to make your own souvenir.

ⓐ Mikiel Azzopardi Street, Siggiewi ⓣ 2146 4931
ⓦ www.limestoneheritage.com ⓔ info@limestoneheritage.com
ⓛ 09.00–16.00 Mon–Fri, 09.00–12.00 Sat–Sun

Mosta Dome (The Church of St Mary)

This church was built between 1833 and 1860. Its portico and triangular gable are based on the Pantheon in Rome, but more famous is its dome, which measures 40 m (122 ft) in internal diameter and has given it its

◐ *Marsaxlokk's photogenic fishing harbour*

Few visitors leave Marsaxlokk without taking a picture of the traditional Maltese fishing boat, the *luzzu* (pronounced 'lut-sue'). Each *luzzu* is painted on either side of its unusually high prow with

its own pair of eyes. This tradition goes back, along with the design of the *luzzu*, to Phoenician times (some 2,500 years ago) when the eye was first painted as a good-luck charm to ward off the dreaded Evil Eye. Ironically, often painted alongside this pagan charm is the name of a Catholic saint.

more familiar name. This is claimed to be the third-largest church dome in the world after St Peter's, in Rome, and St Sophia, in Istanbul.

It is said that the dome was not built so large as an act of deliberate pomposity, but because the church was literally built around an existing church, which could not be demolished until the new one was complete! The interior, lavishly decorated by local artists and trimmed with 18-carat gold leaf, is a marvellous sight. The floor is set with an unusual geometric pattern.

During the Blitz of 1942 it is said that at least two bombs bounced off the dome. A third bomb, however, dropped straight through, while the church was full with some 300 parishioners. By good fortune, bad technology, or – as the Maltese say – by the grace of God, it failed to explode, and so another island miracle was born. A replica of the bomb is displayed in a side room of the church.

Palazzo Parisio

This 19th-century mansion has lavishly decorated ceilings and frescoes, antiques, paintings and bronzes. Its gardens originally stretched for nearly 1 km (½ mile) and today, although smaller, are still impressive.
ⓐ Victory Square, Naxxar ☎ 2141 2461 ⓦ www.palazzoparisio.com
ⓔ info@palazzoparisio.com ❶ Admission charge

San Anton Palace and Gardens

Built by the Grand Master Antoine de Paule, San Anton Palace at Attard is now the Presidential Palace and is not open to the public. You can, however, visit the splendid gardens, laid out in the 17th century, which contain various subtropical trees, such as the banyan.
ⓐ 7 km (4½ miles) south-west of Valletta

The Tarxien Temples & Hypogeum

Located in the midst of a suburb in the town of Tarxien, the Tarxien Temples (pronounced 'Tar-she-en') were built between 3800 and 2500 BC. Stonehenge is about the same age. This is Malta's largest temple complex, and three of its six temples have been partially reconstructed. The Central Temple is the most impressive and was the last to be built. There are many fascinating remains, including altars with animal reliefs, an enormous stone bowl used for ritual purposes, and stone balls thought to have been used to roll the huge stones of the temple into position.

Just 100 m (100 yds) away is Malta's most fascinating temple complex, the subterranean Hypogeum, a unique prehistoric monument in the town of Paola that was discovered accidentally by builders in 1902. Archaeologists found a complex underground system of passages and chambers with carefully crafted masonry arches and columns. The deepest section is 10 m (33 ft) below street level. Wall paintings in delicate red ochre still survive. The Hypogeum is now a UNESCO World Heritage Site. The number of visitors is strictly limited each day, so advance booking is essential.
ⓐ Tarxien Temples and Hypogeum 🕐 07.45–14.00 (16 June–30 Sept); 08.30–16.30 Mon–Sat, 08.30–15.00 Sun (1 Oct–15 June)

● *The Blue Lagoon and view of Comino*

Mediterranean cruise

Located far from the polluting influence of mainland Europe, the blue waters around Malta are some of the clearest and cleanest in the Mediterranean. You cannot say you have truly seen the Maltese archipelago unless you have explored its coastline from the seaboard side at least once. Here is a taste of the tours on offer – check with the tourist office for further details.

THINGS TO SEE & DO

The Blue Lagoon
Not to be confused with the Blue Grotto (see page 86), the glorious waters that divide the island of Comino from the islet of Cominotto are the biggest draw in Maltese cruising. Shallow and sheltered, the waters are not only a lovely inviting colour but they are warm as well. Some trips make this their only destination for the whole day – great if you just want to laze around but with little coastal sightseeing to offer. This idyllic place can become very crowded, which means your boat may anchor a little way out, leaving you a long swim before you can put your feet down – check before you book. The Blue Lagoon is also perfect for scuba diving, and several diving schools run organised trips to here.

Grand Harbour tour
The defence system that protects Valletta and the Three Cities is unquestionably one of the world's greatest feats of military architecture. All the more remarkable is the fact that many of these bastions and fortifications were built over 400 years ago. The only way to appreciate this amazing complex is from the water, on a Grand Harbour tour, with commentary full of lively anecdotes.
🚐 Departs from Sliema ❶ Tours last 90 minutes

Helicopter tour
This is without doubt the most spectacular way of seeing the islands. Viewed from the air, Malta takes on a completely new dimension – often

cluttered and untidy at ground level, the island seems neat and well ordered from the air, especially the grid-pattern streets of Valletta. Other highlights include Grand Harbour, Mdina, Victoria (Gozo) and the Blue Lagoon. Trips take off from the international airport and, with just a 30-minute check-in, there is a minimum of fuss and delay. Helicopter trips last either 20 or 40 minutes. The former covers just Malta, the latter also goes to Gozo. Time in the air quite literally flies by, so the longer trip is recommended if you can afford it.

Do the Oki-Koki

The Oki-Koki speedboats of the Blue Lagoon are great fun, due in no small part to the irrepressible characters who pilot them. They will collect you from your boat, take you on a short but very high-speed thrill ride, then slow down to a sea-snail's pace as you explore the caves. These compare favourably with Malta's famous Blue Grotto (see page 86).

The 'Round Malta' cruise

Departing from Sliema, this tour takes you clockwise around the island, to the picturesque fishing village of Marsaxlokk (see page 78), and the less-than-picturesque industrial Malta Freeport. The tour continues past the famous Blue Grotto (see page 86), dramatic Dingli Cliffs (see page 89), the sandy beaches of Golden Bay (see page 29) and the strange sight of Sweethaven Village (see page 35). A leisurely stop is made in the Blue Lagoon for a swim and the option of 'doing the Oki-Koki' (see above). Lunch is served on board, then it's off to Sliema via St Paul's Bay and the little islands where the Apostle was allegedly shipwrecked.

Sailing cruise

Most cruise boats are motorised. If you would prefer a more romantic voyage, try the *Fernandes* or the *Hera*, beautiful Turkish *gulets* (pronounced 'goo-let') or the fully rigged 70-year-old schooner, *Charlotte Louise*. Combining old-fashioned sail and sleek modernity is the *Spirit of Malta* (summer only), bringing a touch of the Caribbean to Malta, with its lively music and unrationed rum. Most cruises return by 18.00, but

◆ *There is a lot of good diving along the coast of Malta*

when the sun goes down the fun begins on the 'Fernandes Sunday Sunset Cruise' and the 'Spirit of Malta Party Night'.

Underwater safari

If you would like to see what is going on beneath the waves, but you would rather not get your feet wet, or have to struggle into a wetsuit and snorkel, then the Underwater Safari is the cruise for you.

Tour boats operating out of Sliema and Bugibba have a specially designed observation keel below sea level, which seats 38 passengers and allows unimpaired views of some of the clearest and cleanest waters in the Mediterranean.

There are no tropical colours or coral reefs down here, but a generous sprinkling of fish food ensures an abundant following, and an expert marine biologist provides a commentary throughout the tour. On the Bugibba safari, you will also see two wrecks: HMS *Kingston* was sent to the bottom during World War II, whereas the MV *Hanini*, built in Scotland in 1924, was sunk deliberately as an artificial reef to attract fish.

The Blue Grotto & the south-west

The south-west coast of the island is well known for its rugged rocky scenery. The Blue Grotto is Malta's most famous natural formation but the cliffs of Dingli are the most spectacular. Between these lie the island's most dramatically sited temples.

THINGS TO SEE & DO

The Blue Grotto

The Blue Grotto is the biggest and best of a series of sea caves and archways near the village of Zurrieq (pronounced 'Zur-ree-ay'). Small boats pick up passengers in the sheltered picturesque rocky inlet of Wied-iz-Zurrieq and take them on a 25-minute tour. The eroded limestone grottoes and arches are awesome in scale, and the effect of sunlight on the water is magical. The water is brilliantly clear and in the caves it takes on a deep blue hue as the sunlight reflects off the caves and back into the water. Put your hand in the water and even it will look blue!

Buskett Gardens

Most of Malta's trees were cut down a long time ago by medieval shipbuilders, and Buskett Gardens is the only reminder today that this was once a wooded island. The term 'gardens' is, in fact, a bit of a misnomer, as most of this area consists simply of woodland. Not surprisingly, given its rarity value, it is a popular place for picnics, and on 29 June (the feast of St Peter and St Paul – also known as *Mnarja*, pronounced 'Im-nar-yah'), thousands of people come here to celebrate.

The attractions of the area have also long been appreciated by Maltese rulers. On the edge of Buskett Gardens is Verdala Palace, built in 1586 as a summer residence for the Grand Master of the Knights of St John. Today it is the summer house of the President of Malta.

🔺 *The Blue Grotto*

⬤ *The standing stones of Hagar Qim*

Dingli Cliffs

Malta's highest point is 250 m (830 ft) above sea level, measured from the very edge of Dingli Cliffs down the sheer cliff face to the sea. Even on this sheer face, farmers have managed to cultivate some tiny terraces.

The Dingli Cliffs cover virtually the entire southern coast of Malta. The normal sightseeing route is to drive to Rabat and then on to the village of Dingli; the cliffs are 1 km (½ mile) or so beyond the village.

Close to Dingli Cliffs is one of Malta's strangest mysteries. Cut into the flat rocky surface of the ground are long parallel grooves, rather like old tramlines. It is thought that these may have acted as runners for early carts, and are often referred to as cart ruts. The area near Dingli, where these are to be found in large numbers, is known as Clapham Junction.

Hagar Qim and Mnajdra

These two adjacent temple complexes are among the most impressive prehistoric monuments on Malta. Both are around 4,500 to 5,000 years old. The first site you will visit is Hagar Qim (pronounced 'Aa-jah eem'). Its name translates as 'standing stones', for very obvious reasons – one of its giant slabs alone measures 3 m by 7.5 m (9 ft by 23 ft). It is in better condition than its neighbour Mnajdra (pronounced 'Im-nah-ee-dra'), which was vandalized and seriously damaged a few years ago. Both were shrines to Mother Earth, and one school of thought was that the dead would only return to her womb if sacrifices were made at these places. Certainly offerings of animals' blood and milk were made at both temples.

Mnajdra looks on to the smallest of the Maltese islands, Filfla, a tiny rock which may have had a ritual importance once upon a time, though it was used by the British navy for target practice in more recent times. Today it is uninhabited and is protected as a bird reserve.

If you want a good place to cool off on this stretch of coast, you can't beat Ghar Lapsi, a superb natural lido, which is usually only frequented by locals. It is located around 6.5 km (4 miles) due west of Hagar Qim and Mnajdra.

Wine tourism

Malta has an ideal climate for growing grapes and there is a flourishing wine production industry, though not on the scale of Italy, France or Spain. Wine bars are a growth industry all over the islands and there is a demand for assured high-quality wine from Malta's own vineyards, spurred on by an increase in tariff-free imports of French and Italian wine since Malta joined the European Union. Maltese wine makers also produce wine from grapes imported from Italy.

Finding out about Malta's wine-making industry is an entertaining way of spending time away from the beach. Guided tours of wineries and cellars are available at some of the wine makers' premises and you can take part in tutored wine tasting sessions. The vineyards make an attractive scene in some otherwise dull pieces of countryside.

Chardonnay, Syrah and Cabernet Franc are the most common grape varieties grown in Malta and Gozo, but there are also two varieties that are unique to the islands, the white Girgentina (which produces crisp dry white wine) and red Gellewza grapes (which produce fruity medium-bodied red and fine rosé wines). Harvesting takes place by hand in August, earlier than in other countries because the grapes ripen more quickly in Malta's hot humid climate. To increase the growing of grapes in Malta and meet the demand for locally produced wine, the government has made vines a priority agricultural crop, and farmers can get subsidies if they work with wine makers and use their land for growing grapes.

Emanuel Delicata

Delicata is the largest producer of Maltese wine and the originator of an annual wine festival in Valletta at the beginning of August and on Gozo at the end of August. Visitors are welcome at Delicata's 17th-century cellars which have tasting vaults and regular tutored tastings. Phone or email to enquire and make a reservation.

ⓐ The Winery on the Waterfront, Paola ⓣ 2182 5199
ⓦ www.delicata.com ⓔ info@delicata.com

⬥ *Delicata's vineyards stretch out below the town of Mdina*

Marsovin

The best-known producer of Maltese wine is Marsovin, which has five vineyard estates in various parts of the islands, including one on Gozo. The Marsovin winery has cellars that were originally built around 1620 as workshops and stores for the docks in the Grand Harbour. Book a cellar tour by phone or through the Marsovin website.

ⓐ The Winery, Wills Street, Marsa, Paola ❶ 2182 49200
ⓦ www.marsovin.com ❶ Visits by appointment

Meridiana

The Ta'Qali Wine Estate was planted in 1994 and 1995 with Chardonnay, Cabernet Sauvignon, Merlot, Syrah and Petit Verdot grape vines. Meridiana's wine cellars are constructed in local architectural traditional style about 4 m (13 ft) below ground, where the temperature is kept between 18° and 22°C (64° and 72°F). The cellar shop sells a selection of wine and merchandise. ⓐ Meridiana Wine Estate, Ta'Qali ❶ 2141 3550
ⓦ www.meridiana.com.mt ⓔ info@meridiana.com.mt ❶ Cellar shop 09.00–16.00 Mon–Fri, 10.00–12.00 Sat ❶ Tours by appointment

Dacoutros

John Dacoutros & Sons are an old-established wine trading family. The winery has a grape-pressing house with ultramodern pressing facilities, a new barrel room for wine ageing and a fully automated wine, spirit and spumante bottling plant.

ⓐ Winemaker's Wharf, Marsa ❶ 2126 1307 ⓦ www. dacoutros.com
ⓔ info@dacoutros.com ❶ Winery visits and tasting by appointment

Camilleri Winery

Camilleri is a small specialist producer of premium wines from grapes grown entirely in Malta, and holds wine tastings at its retail outlets.

ⓐ Master Wine Buildings, Oratory Street, Naxxar ❶ 2141 2391
ⓦ www.masterwinegroup.com ⓔ info@masterwinegroup.com

❶ *The pretty fishing harbour at Marsaxlokk*

○ As on most islands, fish is always on the menu!

Food & drink

There are few establishments in the tourist resorts that serve exclusively Maltese cuisine. Many restaurants serve a handful of Maltese dishes but alongside these you will find Italian and other international dishes on the menu. Italian is the most common style of restaurant on the island.

FOR STARTERS

Every Mediterranean country has a fish soup and Malta is no exception; here it is called *alijotta*. The most common soup is *minestra*, made of a host of different vegetables, like Italian minestrone. If you are a pasta fan, try the Italian-inspired *ravjul* (ravioli filled with cheese). A very typical Maltese cheese dish is *gbejniet* (or *gbejna*), a pungent round of peppered ewe's-milk cheese, usually served with salad.

FISH DISHES

These will vary by season and availability within the restaurant, but typical fish dishes to look out for are *acciola* (amberjack), *cerna* (grouper), *espadon*, *pixxispad* or *pesce espada* (all names for swordfish) and *lampuki* (dorado). The latter is a Maltese speciality, and is in season from September to November. It is often served in a pie (*torta tal-lampuki*) mixed with tomatoes, onions, olives and various other vegetables. A much more robust-tasting speciality is swordfish Maltese style, smothered in a tasty sauce of tomatoes and capers. Another enjoyable local seafood dish is octopus, often served in a dark tomato sauce. Other unusual fish names you may come across are *dott* (stone bass) and *dentici* (sea bream).

RABBIT

The islanders' favourite meat dish is *fenek* (rabbit). This may be served *biz-zalza* (casseroled) or fried. Rabbit is the Maltese celebration dish, and a traditional *fenkata* evening usually comprises a menu of spaghetti with rabbit sauce, followed by roast rabbit, then by nuts and figs. As a special treat it may be served as a pie (*torta tal-fenek*) with pork, peas, tomatoes and other ingredients. You will have to use your fingers to get the bones out of the rabbit, but the dish is tasty and justifies the effort.

MORE MEAT DISHES

Aside from rabbit, the other classic Maltese meat dish is *bragioli*, made from a flattened beef fillet, stuffed with bacon, breadcrumbs and hard-boiled eggs, rolled up and simmered in wine with onions. Less common on restaurant menus are Maltese sausages, which are of the familiar British link variety (as opposed to the continental slicing style). Often flavoured with lemon and herbs, these are delicious.

CHEESE AND PASTA

Two favourite national dishes which strongly reflect the Italian influence are *timpana* – baked macaroni with meat, eggs and cheese (and perhaps peas and aubergines), topped with flaky pastry – and *ross-fil-forn* –

⬤ *Olive oil – a staple ingredient in Mediterranean cooking and the perfect accompaniment to bread*

savoury rice, baked with eggs and meat. You may also find these sold from street stalls in square containers as takeaway snacks.

SNACKS

Typical Maltese snacks are sold in cafés or street kiosks. The ubiquitous lunchtime filler is *hobz biz zejt*, which translates as 'bread with oil'. This is a delicious, typically Mediterranean, snack of bread smeared with a paste of tomatoes, garlic, capers and olive oil, then filled with tuna, olives and salad. It may also be served toasted (like Italian bruschetta) as a starter in restaurants. Some places advertise *hobz biz zejt* as 'Maltese Bread'.

A favourite morning snack is a *pastizzi rikotta* (flaky ricotta-cheese envelope) or a *qassatat* (pronounced 'ass-er-tat'), a round flaky or shortcrust pie, filled either with cheese or yellow marrowfat peas. The latter is sometimes referred to as *pizelli*. Both are sold fresh from the oven, and are best eaten warm.

SWEET THINGS

The Maltese have a sweet tooth and it is always a treat to pop into a *pastizzerija* for a coffee, pastry or other confections on offer. Nougat is very popular and nougat vendors are an integral part of the village *festa*.

DRINKS

The Maltese have inherited coffee from the Italians and tea from the British, but coffee is nearly always a better bet. The British have also bequeathed to the Maltese a dark, cold, fizzy, pale ale, sold almost everywhere under the Hopleaf brand. Cisk Lager (pronounced 'Chisk') is its companion brew. Maltese wines have come on in leaps and bounds in recent years, and good-quality Maltese wines are excellent. Gozo makes its own wines, which are gutsy and with a higher than average alcohol content. The national soft drink is Kinnie, a refreshing fizzy drink, flavoured with bitter oranges and aromatic herbs.

Menu decoder

Most restaurants in Malta serve international food, but you may come across the following Maltese specialities in bakers' shops, street stalls or rural cafés.

alijotta Fish soup, powerfully packed with garlic.

kabocci mimlija Cabbage leaves stuffed with minced beef or cheese.

kanolli ta-rrikotta Croissants stuffed with ricotta cheese blended with chocolate, almonds and preserved cherries.

kappunata Similar to ratatouille, a vegetable stew made with aubergines, peppers, onions, tomatoes and courgettes, flavoured with garlic and capers.

kinnie A bitter but refreshing local drink made from oranges and wormwood (a type of herb).

mqarets Deep-fried date pastries, which are part of the island's Arab legacy. Their tempting aroma wafts around the main gate to Valletta.

pastizzi Puff-pastry pasties stuffed with mashed peas and spices or ricotta cheese.

ravjul Ravioli with a difference – stuffed with locally made ricotta cheese.

timpana Another traditional pie, this time of Sicilian origin, made from minced beef, potatoes, eggs and pasta in a white sauce.

torta tal lampuki A traditional pie of Arabic origin (blending sweet and savoury ingredients) eaten as a summer snack; different cooks have different recipes combining *lampuki* (also known as *dorado* – a meaty white fish similar to mackerel) with some or all of the following: spinach, puréed cauliflower, onions, garlic, tomatoes, chestnuts and sultanas.

◆ *One of Malta's daily pleasures is dining* alfresco *with a sea view*

Shopping

CRAFTS VILLAGES
For the best range of Maltese handicrafts – lace, filigree jewellery, chunky woollen jumpers, woodwork, metalwork, glass and so on – try the **Ta'Qali Crafts Village**, on Malta, where you can watch local artisans at work, or the smaller complex of **Ta'Dbiegi**, just outside San Lawrenz, on Gozo (see page 74).

GLASSWARE
Glass is the island's most striking product, often produced in beautiful hues of gold and brown or blue. Maltese and Gozitan blown glass is not cheap, but the quality is high and you can watch the pieces being made.

LACE
Lace is the island speciality. Look out for tablecloths, napkins, shawls and handkerchiefs. Lacemakers are literally a dying breed on the islands, and if you are not buying from a traditional outlet, where you can see artisans at work, watch out for imitations imported from the Far East.

MARKETS
The markets in Valletta are the best on the island. The Sunday-morning market, known as the Monti, just outside the City Gate, has an interesting flea-market section but is mostly full of tourist fare and counterfeit products from the Far East. There is a lively bustle to the market, and it is worth a visit to see a slice of everyday Maltese life. The daily market on Triq Mercanti/Merchants' Street features much the same style of merchandise. Pop into the indoor market on the same street to catch the colourful fruit and vegetable stands and delicatessens.

SILVER & GOLD
More portable than glass, and often just as beautiful, is the delicate filigree silver and gold jewellery produced by Maltese artisans. You can see them at work in many places and prices are often competitive.

VALLETTA

Valletta is not so much for shoppers as shop lovers. Here you will still find small specialist shops with beautiful facades that have survived, virtually untouched, since the 1940s. This is the place to buy silver filigree jewellery, Maltese stamps, glassware and other island specialities from enthusiastic shop owners who know their business inside out.

WINTER WOOLLIES

If the weather turns cold, or the wind blows hard, you'll appreciate the islands' woollens, particularly the chunky Aran-style knitted jumpers that are a speciality of Gozo. Prices are very reasonable.

🔺 *There are many markets that are fun to browse around*

Children

HORSE RIDING

If they are old enough to hold on, then they are probably old enough to ride a horse at the Golden Bay Horse Riding stables (see page 29). The owners are very friendly, are accustomed to dealing with children and use special safety harnesses to prevent accidents.

MEDITERRANEO MARINE PARK

Next door to Splash & Fun Water Park (combined tickets are available for both facilities) the entertainment includes shows with sea lions, turtles, parrots and cockatoos, but the park's real stars are the dolphins, rescued from the Black Sea, who perform crowd-pleasing stunts. But more than that, adults and children over eight can have the thrill of a lifetime by getting wet and swimming with the dolphins. ❶ 2137 2218
Ⓦ www.mediterraneo.com.mt ❷ mediterraneo@waldonet.net.mt
🕐 10.00–15.30 Apr–Oct, 10.00–16.30 Nov–Mar except Mon
❶ Advance booking essential. At least three weeks' notice is usually required

PLAYMOBIL FUNPARK

See around the Playmobil factory and watch the toys being made. Outside there are hours of fun to be had playing in a Playmobil park.
ⓐ HF80, Industrial Estate, Hal Far ❶ 2224 2445
Ⓦ www.playmobilmalta.com 🕐 10.00–18.00 Mon–Sat, 10.00–13.00 Sun (July–Sept); 10.00–18.00 daily (winter)

SPLASH & FUN WATER PARK

Water slides and tubes, jets, pipe falls, water guns, a wave pool – just about everything for fun in the water. Don't miss the Lazy River (an inflatable ring through cascading waterfalls) or the Space Bowl (a thrilling dark tube that sends you round and round a large bowl before you drop into the pool below). ⓐ Located on the main coast road between St Julian's and St Paul's Bay at Bahar Ic-Caghaq (just ask the

bus driver for Splash & Fun) ☎ 2137 4283 🌐 www.splashandfun.com.mt
✉ info@splashandfun.com.mt 🕐 10.00–19.00 mid-May to mid-Sept

YOUNG TEENAGERS

Pack your children off to one of the special, alcohol-free, early-evening weekend discos in Paceville (at St Julian's), or make a family visit to the tenpin bowling alleys at **Eden Super Bowl**, at St George's Bay. If the thought of Mdina, the Silent City, doesn't appeal, tell them about **Mdina Dungeon** – gruesome waxworks of actual medieval horrors (see page 60).

⬤ *The fantastic slides at Splash & Fun Water Park*

Sports & activities

HORSE RIDING

The friendly, helpful Golden Bay riding centre (see page 29) is equally at home with experienced riders and complete novices. You can ride for one or two hours, following trails along the coastal paths and overlooking the beaches, among some of the island's least-spoiled countryside.
🕿 2157 3360 ❶ Book ahead

MARSA SPORTS CENTRE

Right in the centre of the island, the Marsa Sports complex offers a wide range of activities. This includes the only golf course on Malta – the 18-hole Royal Malta Club (equipment is for hire) – 17 tennis courts, 5 squash courts, mini-golf, an open-air swimming pool and billiards.

◔ Mellieha is excellent for watersports

TYPICALLY MALTESE

Horse racing, of the trotting variety, is the most popular spectator sport in Malta. Jockeys do not ride the horses but are pulled along behind on a flimsy-looking trap. The track is at Marsa (public buses and organised excursions run there) and meetings on winter Sundays pull in large crowds. Racing continues throughout most of the year. You can enjoy a flutter on the tote or with the course bookies. The other Maltese sporting speciality is waterpolo. You can see top-quality league games staged in the 'pitches' on the seafront at several places including Sliema, St Paul's Bay and St Julian's, on summer weekends. ● See local papers for details of fixtures

WALKING

March to June, and October are the best months for walking in Malta and Gozo. The latter is particularly pleasant as there is more unspoiled countryside to ramble. Ask at the tourist office for a local guide to take you out, or, alternatively, do it yourself with the assistance of *Hiking in Malta, Gozo & Comino*, published by J. Kolb Publishing (mostly aimed at experienced walkers), available at bookshops in Valletta, if not in your resort.

WATERSPORTS

The island's clear blue waters and warm summer seas (averaging 23°C/73.5°F) mean that diving is a very popular pastime. The scarcity of sand, lack of pollution and stillness of the virtually tide-free waters all contribute to excellent visibility, which on average is up to 30 m (100 ft). You won't see too many exotic fish, but there are caves and grottoes to explore, and good wreck diving. Most clubs on the island operate to a high standard, are PADI and BSAC affiliated, and are well equipped to deal with beginners and experienced divers.

At Golden Bay, Mellieha Bay, and at various lidos around the island, you will find the usual range of resort watersports, including windsurfing (the conditions at Mellieha are excellent), waterskiing and jet skis.

Festivals & events

CARNIVAL

Held in the week before Lent (usually around late February), this is one of the most colourful events of the Maltese festival calendar. It culminates in a procession of floats featuring grotesque characters with giant heads. Open-air dancing competitions are also held. Festivities take place in various locations, though the main ones are in Valletta and just outside, at Floriana.

FESTA

The island's most visual cultural celebration is the village *festa*, or festival. The purpose of the *festa* is to honour the village patron saint. Various events, mostly of a religious nature, are conducted from Wednesday through to Sunday. The religious highlight is the Sunday night procession, when a weighty statue of the saint is carried shoulder high by sturdy villagers.

The whole village will be festooned with banners, and the centrepiece is the church, gloriously decorated with hundreds of coloured lights outside and with sumptuous red damask inside. Other buildings, such as the village band club, will also be lavishly decorated.

The village brass band, and possibly visiting brass bands, parade and play, and, on Saturday night, singers may join in to perform an outdoor concert in the village square.

Traditional Maltese nougat is sold from gleaming, portable wood-and-glass cabinets, and there are fast-food vendors too. Saturday night climaxes with a marvellous display of powerful set-piece fireworks on large wooden stands dotted around the village centre. Aerial fireworks are saved until the sun sets, and they bring the *festa* to a spectacular finale.

The *festa* season begins in mid-April and lasts until September, with at least one festival taking place somewhere each week.

◯ Festa *night*

🔺 *Religious procession*

THE PERFORMING ARTS

For an evening of conventional high culture, visit Valletta's Manoel Theatre. This little gem stages regular productions of ballet, opera, concerts and plays. Look in the local paper to see what is on. A free lunchtime concert is held in one of the theatre's recital rooms every Wednesday.

The Luxol Stadium and Parade Ground in Pembroke host major popular music concerts. Big names such as Bryan Adams, Sting and Pink Floyd have performed there. During the annual Arts Festival in July and August, opera singers perform in front of historic monuments and in Mdina's main square with the Cathedral as a backdrop.

▶ *The ferry crossing to Gozo*

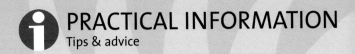

PRACTICAL INFORMATION

Accommodation

Malta has a vast range of hotels and apartments. Prices are very competitive, but of course the best deals are found outside the high season. The hotels below are graded by approximate price:

£ = budget   **££** = mid-range   **£££** = expensive

BUGIBBA & QAWRA

Bugibba Holiday Complex £ Part hotel, part self-catering apartments in the heart of the Bugibba resort, with its own supermarket, Jacks Bar, Terrazza poolside snack bar, a pizzeria and a buffet restaurant. 🅐 Tourist Street, Bugibba 🌐 2158 0861 🆆 www.islandhotels.com

Coastline Hotel ££ Large resort hotel overlooking Salina Bay, near Bugibba and St Paul's Bay. The health and leisure centre has a gymnasium, sauna, heated jet pool and a massage treatment room. 🅐 Salina Bay 🌐 2157 3781 🆆 www.coastline.com.mt

Park Lane ££ An aparthotel combining the freedom of self-catering apartments with the service of a hotel. Located close to the bus station, pubs and restaurants. 🅐 Maskli Street, Qawra 🌐 2157 7319 🅔 info@parklanemalta.com

San Antonio ££ Large hotel complex with extensive grounds, including a pool and sun terraces fringed with palm trees. Excellent fitness and spa treatment facilities and a choice of restaurants – The Costa, Bonaparte Brasserie and Oliver's Coffee Shop. 🅐 Qawra 🌐 2158 3434 🆆 www.sanantonio-malta.com 🅔 info@sanantonio-malta.com

Suncrest Hotel ££ Large hotel on the promenade with its own lido, the Sun and Surf beach club by the sea, accessed by a tunnel under the road. Has a choice of dining, with the first class restaurant, It-Tokk, serving Mediterranean and Maltese dishes; a buffet dining room,

Le Pavillion; and pizzeria, Tal-Kaptan. ⓐ Qawra Coas Road, Qawra
ⓣ 2157 7101 ⓦ www.suncresthotel.com
ⓔ reservations@suncresthotel.com

MDINA
Xara Palace £££ The only hotel within the city of Mdina. An up-market elegant hotel in a restored 17th-century building set within Mdina's medieval walls. ⓐ The Xara Palace Relais and Chateaux, Misrah il-Kunsill, Mdina ⓣ 2145 0560 ⓦ www.xarapalace.com.mt

MELLIEHA
Solana ££ Value-for-money hotel in a low-rise limestone building with its own swimming pool and a roof-top hydro-massage pool. Some rooms have a view over to Gozo and Comino and the ferry is close by. ⓐ Gorg Borg Olivier Street, Mellieha ⓣ 2152 2209 ⓦ www.solanahotel.com.mt

ST JULIAN'S & PACEVILLE
Hotel Bernard £ Comfortable modern hotel in the heart of the nightclub capital of Malta, a short walk from the beach of St George's Bay and directly across the road from the Bay Street complex. The Red Aroma Restaurant and O'Casey's Irish pub are in the same building. ⓐ St George's Bay ⓣ 2137 3900 ⓦ www.hotelsmalta.com

Bay Street Hotel ££ A large hotel (has 100 en suite rooms) close to the action in Paceville. The hotel reception is reached through the Bay Street tourist shopping complex. Buffet breakfast is served in the All Seasons Restaurant on the fourth floor. Roof-top swimming pool on the seventh floor. ⓐ St George's Bay ⓣ 2138 4421 ⓦ www.baystreet.com.mt

ST PAUL'S BAY
San Pawl Hotel £ Good value family hotel in a quiet residential area within a few minutes' walk from the old village of St Paul's Bay and the

resorts of Bugibba and Qawra. Outdoor and indoor pools. ⓐ Blacktail Street, St Paul's Bay ① 2157 1752 ⓦ www.sanpawlhotel.com ⓔ info@sanpawlhotel.com

Ambassador ££ Good value modern hotel on the water's edge on the Xemxija side of St Paul's Bay. Large seawater pool and Internet café. ⓐ Shipwreck Promenade, Xemxija, St Paul's Bay ① 2157 3870 ⓦ www.ambassadormalta.com ⓔ info@ambassadormalta.com

Gillieru Harbour Hotel ££ Small family-run hotel on the water's edge with views over the bay to St Paul's islands. Very convenient for shops and the promenade. ⓐ Church Square, St Paul's Bay ① 2157 2720 ⓦ www.gillieru.com ⓔ gillieru@maltanet.net

Karanne Hotel ££ Large aparthotel with a choice of apartments or full-service hotel rooms, near the harbour. Four rooms are specially adapted for people with reduced mobility. ⓐ Blacktail Street, St Paul's Bay ① 2158 3777 ⓦ www.karanne.com ⓔ reservations@karanne.net

SLIEMA
Europa £ This well-located, value-for-money hotel on the seafront in central Sliema is run by a friendly young team. The trendy Long Island Lounge bar serves cocktails and snacks and the Europa has its own in-house sushi bar. ⓐ 138 Tower Road, Sliema ① 2133 4070 ⓦ www.europahotel-malta.com

Imperial Hotel ££ Comfortable and reasonably priced large hotel with a feeling of past grandeur. Swimming pool and Internet access. ⓐ Rudolf Street, Sliema ① 2134 4093 ⓦ www.imperialhotelmalta.com

Fortuna Spa Resort £££ Ultimate luxury on Sliema's seafront, with spa facilities in the privacy of your bedroom. Some rooms have a their own roof garden. ⓐ Tigne Seafront ① 2346 0000 ⓦ www.hotelfortina.com

Preparing to go

GETTING THERE

The cheapest way to get to Malta is to book a package holiday with one of the leading tour operators. The flight time from Britain to Malta is just over three hours. The national airline, Air Malta, has daily flights from London and regular flights from regional airports around Britain including Liverpool. British Airways flies to Malta from Gatwick and Manchester. Low fares airlines have opened up Malta as a short-break destination. Ryanair flies direct to Malta International from London Luton and Dublin. The Swiss-owned low-fares airline British Jet has flights from London Gatwick and Stansted and ten regional airports in Britain including Birmingham, Cardiff, Glasgow, Manchester and Norwich. GB Airways operates daily flights to Malta from Gatwick and Manchester. Charter flights from Gatwick and various regional airports in Britain are available from Thomas Cook Airlines, XL.com, First Choice Airways and Thomson Holidays. All these airlines have partnerships with hotels and can provide good-value package deals all year.

If your travelling times are flexible, and if you can avoid the school holidays, you can also find some very cheap last-minute deals using the websites of the leading holiday companies.

BEFORE YOU LEAVE

Holidays should be about fun and relaxation, so avoid last-minute panics and stress by making your preparations well in advance.

MALTA TOURIST OFFICE

Further information about Malta can be obtained from the Malta Tourist Office ⓐ Unit C Parkhouse, 14 Northfields, London SW18 1DD
ⓣ 020 8877 6990 ⓕ 020 8874 9416 ⓦ www.visitmalta.com
The Malta Tourism Authority has information offices at:
Malta International Airport ⓐ Arrivals Lounge ⓣ 2369 6073
ⓛ 10.00–21.00

Valletta ⓐ 1 City Arcades, City Gate ☏ 2123 7350 🕐 08.30–18.00 Mon–Sat, 08.30–14.00 Sun
St Julian's ⓐ Spinola Palace, Spinola Bay ☏ 2316 0420 🕐 10.00–21.00
Victoria (Gozo) ⓐ Tigrija Palazz, Republic Street ☏ 2156 1419
🕐 09.00–12.30 and 13.00–17.00 (closed Sun pm)

DOCUMENTS

The most important documents you will need are your tickets and your passport. Check well in advance that your passport is up to date and has at least three months left to run (six months is even better). All children, including newborn babies, need their own passport now, unless they are already included on the passport of the person they are travelling with. It generally takes at least a week to process a passport renewal. This can be longer in the run-up to the summer months. For the latest information on how to renew your passport and the processing times call the **Passport Agency** on ☏ 0870 521 0410 or ⓦ www.ukpa.gov.uk

You should check the details of your travel tickets well before your departure, ensuring that the timings and dates are correct.

If you are thinking of hiring a car while you are away, you will need to have your driving licence with you. If you want more than one driver for the car, the other drivers must have their licence too.

MONEY

Malta is a member state of the European Union and the euro is the national currency. All major credit cards are acceptable in Malta for shopping and paying hotel bills, except for in the smallest establishments. Cash machines (ATMs) are plentiful in the main cities and towns so you can take money out using a debit card, Visa, Mastercard, Cirrus or Link card.

Traveller's cheques have rather fallen out of favour since credit cards became the main method of paying bills in hotels and restaurants, and you will need to go to a main bank branch or to a Thomas Cook office to exchange them for cash.

INSURANCE

Have you got sufficient cover for your holiday? Check that your policy covers you for loss of possessions and valuables, for activities you might want to try – such as scuba-diving, horse-riding, or watersports – and for emergency medical and dental treatment, and flights home if required.

CLIMATE

The hot months are from June to September when the average daytime temperature reaches 32°C (89°F) and there is little rain. Sea breezes bring welcome relief, but Malta is also subject to the hot humid *xlokk* or sirocco winds that blow from the Sahara Desert. October is still warm and sunny but rainfall is frequent. The winter months can be cold and wet, but are still mild compared to northern Europe. Springtime is warm and sunny and can be the best time to visit Malta.

AIRPORT PARKING & ACCOMMODATION

If you intend to leave your car in an airport car park while you are away, or stay the night at an airport hotel before or after your flight, you should book well ahead to take advantage of hotel discounts or cheap off-airport parking. Airport accommodation gets booked up several weeks in advance, especially during the height of the holiday season. Check whether the hotel offers free parking for the duration of the holiday.

PACKING TIPS

Baggage allowances vary according to the airline, destination and the class of travel, but 20 kg (44 lb) per person is the norm for luggage that is carried in the hold (it usually tells you what the weight limit is on your ticket). You are also allowed one item of cabin baggage weighing no more than 5 kg (11 lb), and measuring 46 by 30 by 23 cm (18 by 12 by 9 in). A handbag counts as one item.

   In addition, you can carry your airport purchases as hand baggage. Large items – surfboards, golf clubs, collapsible wheelchairs and pushchairs – are usually charged as extras – let the airline know in advance that you want to bring these.

CHECK-IN, PASSPORT CONTROL & CUSTOMS

Allow yourself plenty of time for airport security checks, which can be lengthy, especially in the busy summer months. All metal objects, electronic devices such as iPods, MP3 players and laptop computers, coats and jackets must be placed in trays for scanning in the X-ray machines. You may also be required to take off your shoes and put them through the scanner as an additional, random, security check.

Liquids and gels such as sun-tan lotion and toothpaste that you want to take in your carry-on bag must be in containers no larger than 100 ml and placed in a clear plastic bag for inspection. Larger liquid items must be in your checked-in luggage or they will be confiscated.

You are restricted to only one item of carry-on baggage and it must be small enough to fit into the overhead storage bins in the aircraft cabin. A handbag counts as one item, so if you want to take another bag through, you should place the handbag inside it.

There are no Customs restrictions on alcohol and tobacco when travelling between Malta and other countries of the EU, but you should be aware that there is no duty-free allowance either. Prohibited items include firearms, pornography, meat, poultry and their by-products, plants and recreational drugs.

Entry or transit visas are not required for stays of up to three months for holidays or unpaid business trips by nationals of most Commonwealth countries, UK dependencies or European Union countries. If a stay of longer than three months is planned, applications should be made in person, before the end of the initial three-month period, to the Principal Immigration Officer, Immigration Police, Police Headquarters, Floriana.

Nationals of countries that require a visa should obtain these from a Maltese embassy or consulate. Where neither of these is available, a written request should be made to the Commissioner of Police, Police Headquarters, Floriana – faxed applications are acceptable ❶ 2124 7777. Application forms can also be downloaded from ⓦ www.foreign.gov.mt

Visitors requiring an entry visa to Malta and who undertake day trips (of less than 24 hours) to another country are exempted from paying another entry visa on their return to Malta.

During your stay

AIRPORTS

Malta International Airport is located next to the village of Gudja, 10 km (6 miles) from Valletta.

Land-side facilities at MIA include airline ticketing offices and aviation counter, baby-care rooms, two banks, cafeterias, car hire offices, chapel, pharmacist, flight information counter, florist, international telephone, lotto booth, newsagent, post office, restaurant, sweets shop, telecommunications centre, tourist information counter and a viewing gallery.

Air-side facilities include baby-care facilities, bar/cafeteria, duty-free shops – in both arrivals and departure halls – and three VIP/executive lounges (the Ewropa Lounge is operated by Air Malta, whilst the La Valette Executive and Gerolamo Cassar (arrivals hall) lounges are run by the airport operating company – Malta International Airport plc).

BEACHES

The coastline of the Maltese islands is generally rocky and not renowned for its sandy beaches. The rock generally slopes down very gently for a long way out, and there are no tides or surf on Maltese beaches.

There are several sandy beaches in the north of Malta; the best are Mellieha Bay, Gnejna Bay, Golden Bay, Ghajn Tuffieha and Paradise Bay. In the south, the finest is Pretty Bay in Birzebbugia, and, in Gozo, Ramla Bay stands out for its red sand. Comino has two sandy beaches – Santa Marija Bay and St Nicklaw Bay. Rock bathing is possible at almost all

> **BEACH SAFETY**
> A flag system operates, to advise you of swimming conditions.
> **Red** = dangerous – no swimming at all
> **Yellow** = strong swimmers only – exercise caution
> **Green** = safe bathing conditions for all

other beach sites. In many areas the rocks are flat and worn smooth and can be very slippery. You should take care about rocks under the water which can be jagged and cause a nasty gash if you fall.

An alternative to beach swimming is to use lidos, enclosed pools with decks and sun-beds usually operated by hotels but open to the general public. Some have access to a private stretch of open sea beach.

Malta is striving to have all beaches classified under the EU's Blue Flag system, which is a sign that the beach is safe. A Blue Flag beach will have a lifeguard patrol during the daytime, but many beaches still do not have lifeguards.

CAR HIRE

Renting cars in Malta is the cheapest in Europe. A national driving licence is sufficient. The main international car-hire firms such as Hertz and Avis are represented in the international airport and in the main resorts. Your hotel reception can advise on renting cars from local companies, whose cars are cheaper but not as new. Petrol stations are open only in the daytime and it can be difficult to fill up on Sundays.

Malta is one of Europe's safest destinations. The main danger is theft of possessions from parked cars. Attendants will often look after your car at beaches and archaeological sites. It is customary to give them a small tip (around 10 to 25 cents).

CASINOS

There are four casinos in Malta: the **Dragonara Casino** in St Julian's, the **Casino di Venezia** in Vittoriosa/Birgu, the **Oracle Casino** at the Dolmen Resort Hotel in Qawra and **The Casino** at Portomaso, the new marina complex in St Julian's. You need to produce identity (a passport will do) for admittance. Foreign nationals must be 18 and Maltese citizens 25, and there is requirement for smart casual dress – for men this usually means shirt and tie.

Maltese casinos have high-jackpot slot machines and the full range of table games, including roulette, blackjack and various styles of poker. They also have bars and high-class dining in sumptuous surroundings, and musical entertainment. The Dragonara and Oracle also have courtesy bus services to and from the hotels in the St Julian's and Sliema areas.

ELECTRICITY

The electrical supply is 240 volts, single phase, 50 cycles. The 13-amp, British-style three-pin rectangular sockets are used in Malta.

FACILITIES FOR VISITORS WITH DISABILITIES

Most hotels and visitor attractions now offer facilities for those with disabilities. Entrances and corridors are generally step-free and usually one lift has doors wide enough to take a wheelchair. Public places such as churches, attractions and historic sites have ramps except where this is impossible. If you require assistance at the airport, notify your airline at the time of booking and arrangements can be made at Malta International Airport for your arrival.

GETTING AROUND

Driving

As in many Commonwealth countries, driving in Malta is on the left. There is a speed limit of 80 km/h (50 mph) on highways and 50 km/h (30 mph) in urban areas. Third-party insurance is advisable, as the island's accident rate is one of the highest in Europe. International and national driving licences are acceptable and may be endorsed free to visitors at police headquarters in Floriana (☎ 2122 4001/9).

In the event of an accident, telephone the police on 191 and, if required, an ambulance, on 196. If the collision is severe, drivers should not move cars until the police have arrived and taken note of the incident. Insurance companies will not entertain any claim unless it is supported by a police report. In the event of minor accidents, a form – obtained from any police station – must be completed.

Bus

The Maltese bus service is cheap, efficient and a bit of an adventure. The buses themselves are very old, and on Gozo you can ride the classic

British Leyland Super Comet from the 1950s, which is still in service. Many of the buses are driver-owned and are cleaned and looked after with tender loving care. They all show a route number, but you should check with the driver to be certain where the bus is going as they don't show the destination. You can't always rely on timetables, but most routes run every 20 minutes.

The main bus station for Valletta is immediately outside the main city gate. Sliema waterfront is also an important terminus and there is a bus station in Bugibba/Qawra. Buses to and from Cirkewwa are timed to meet the Gozo ferry, as are the buses at Mgarr Harbour for the drive to Victoria.

A new shuttle-bus service runs direct from the international airport to Cirkewwa for the Gozo ferry and is an economical and efficient alternative to taxis. The journey takes about 40 minutes.

Taxi

It is a common irritation for visitors that Maltese taxi drivers don't always start their meters at the beginning of a journey, so you don't really know how much the trip is going to cost unless you agree it before getting in the car. Taxis are not cheap, so overcharging should not be tolerated. Taxi fares are governed by law, but the law is rarely enforced unless customers complain to the Malta Transport Authority (ⓘ freephone 8007 2393).

Hotel reception staff can call a taxi or a private hire car (usually black) and get the price at the time of booking. Taxis are essential if you go out at night, as the bus services stop at 22.00, apart from a few night buses running from Paceville to the main resorts to cater for the nightclub crowd.

Fares from the international airport are more strictly enforced and you would normally pay in advance at a booth in the Arrivals terminal, and hand a voucher to the taxi driver. Fares from the airport (and the sea passenger terminal) are set. As an indication, expect to pay €14 from the airport to Valletta, €19 to St Julian's, €24 to St Paul's Bay and €31 to Cirkewwa for the Gozo ferry (exact fares are subject to annual review). These rates apply at all times including nights, Sundays and public holidays.

HEALTH MATTERS

There are no particular health hazards in Malta except the risk of sunburn. Tap water is safe to drink but may taste strange to foreigners; bottled water is easy to find in shops and cafés.

No inoculations are required, though a yellow fever certificate is needed if you have been in an infected area.

Malta offers free basic health care to EU citizens on production of a *European Health Insurance Card* (EHIC). This is not a substitute for medical cover on travel insurance and would not cover the costs of a hospital stay or repatriation after a serious illness or accident. Nor does the EHIC entitle you to free ongoing or non-urgent medical treatment, it simply entitles the holder to the level of free medical treatment that locals get. You can apply for an EHIC free of charge online at Ⓦ www.ehic.org.uk or by calling the UK Department of Health, (🕓 0845 606 2030), or by filling in a form from any post office. Malta also has reciprocal health agreements with Australia.

If you are undergoing medical treatment at the time of your visit to Malta, stock up with enough medicine or tablets before you leave.

There are two state-run hospitals in Malta: St Luke's in Guadamagia and Mater Dei in Birkirkarra; and one in Gozo, Gozo General Hospital in Victoria. If you need an ambulance in an emergency, dial 196 in Malta or 2156 0600 in Gozo.

There are dentists in most towns, and all speak English.

INTERNET

Most resorts and hotels have Internet access points and new Internet cafés are opening all the time. Charges for Internet time vary, but expect to pay about €1 per hour.

MEDIA

There are two locally published English-language daily newspapers – the *Malta Independent* and *The Times of Malta* – and both have Sunday editions, along with *Malta Today*. English newspapers are also available from newsagents, usually in the late afternoon on the day of publication.

PRACTICAL INFORMATION

A free English-language listings guide, *Events Malta*, is published monthly and is packed with information.

USEFUL WEBSITES

Air Malta	www.airmalta.com
About Malta	www.aboutmalta.com
Gozo	www.gozo.com
Malta International Airport	www.maltairport.com
Malta Tourism Authority	www.visitmalta.com
Malta Weather	www.maltaweather.com
Search Malta	www.searchmalta.com

OPENING HOURS

Banks

These are generally open 08.30–3.30 Mon–Thur and Fri until 15.30. Many banks now open on Sat mornings until 12.00. There are ATMs (cash machines) in most towns. Exchange traveller's cheques at the main branch of a bank.

Shops

Traditional shop opening hours are 09.00–13.00 and 16.00–19.00, but many shops in resorts stay open all afternoon and some go on until 22.00. In villages, local shopkeepers adhere to the siesta tradition. Most shops close on Sundays and public holidays, except those geared for souvenirs and holiday shopping.

Chemists

Open during normal shopping hours, and have a rota system for Sunday mornings, 09.00–12.30 in Malta and 07.30–11.00 on Gozo.

Bars, cafés and restaurants

Most bars close at 01.00, but in St Julian's and Paceville many bars also act as nightclubs and have longer hours. Restaurants open at 11.30 for lunch but then close in the afternoon and reopen for dinner service at 19.00.

Post offices

Standard post office opening hours are 07.45–13.30 Mon–Fri, and 09.00–12.00 Sat. The main post office at Qormi (ⓐ 305 Qormi Road) and the Gozo post office (ⓐ 129 Republic Street, Victoria) have longer opening hours, from 07.45–18.30 Mon–Sat. Stamps can be bought at hotel receptions.

PUBLIC HOLIDAYS

These can be great fun if you are looking for a party with the locals, but be aware that many shops and historic sites are closed on public holidays.

1 Jan	New Year's Day
10 Feb	Commemoration of St Paul's Shipwreck
19 Mar	Feast of St Joseph
31 Mar	Freedom Day
Mar/Apr	Good Friday and Easter (dates vary)
1 May	Labour Day
7 June	*Sette Giugno*
29 June	St Peter and St Paul (*L-Imnarja*)
15 Aug	Assumption of Our Lady (Santa Marija)
8 Sept	Victory Day, Birthday of the Virgin Mary
21 Sept	Independence Day
8 Dec	Immaculate Conception
25 Dec	Christmas

WHAT TO DO IN AN EMERGENCY

Staff manning the emergency services all speak perfect English.

On Malta Police ☎ 191; Ambulance ☎ 196; Fire ☎ 199
On Gozo Police and fire ☎ 2156 2044; Ambulance ☎ 2156 0600

RELIGION

The majority of Maltese are Roman Catholic. There are small Anglican, Church of Scotland, Greek Catholic and Orthodox, Jewish and Muslim communities.

TELEPHONES

Maltese local telephone numbers are generally eight digits, beginning 21 for land lines and either 79 or 99 for mobiles. For calls into Malta, the country code is 356. To get hold of an international operator, dial 1152, and for local directory enquiries dial 1182.

Malta is fully integrated into the mobile phone roaming network, so you should be able to use your own mobile phone for calling and receiving calls, but at a price.

Most coin-operated public phone boxes can be used only for local calls, but red British-style public phone boxes now accept cards and some are also email enabled. International phone calls can also be made from Internet cafés. There is a 24-hour service of international communications at the Maltacom offices in St George's Bay, St Julian's.

TIME DIFFERENCES

Malta is on Central European Time (CET), one hour ahead of GMT (Universal Time) in winter and two hours from the last Sunday in March until the last Sunday in October. Malta is six hours ahead of Eastern Standard Time (EST), seven in the summertime.

TELEPHONING MALTA

To call Malta from the UK, dial 00 356 then the eight-digit number – there's no need to wait for a dialling tone.

TELEPHONING ABROAD

To call an overseas number from Malta, dial 00 followed by the country code (UK = 44), then the area code (minus the initial 0) and then the number you want.

A

accommodation 110–11
airports and air travel 113, 115–16, 117
Armier Bay 32
ATMs 114

B

baggage allowances 115, 116
banks 121
beaches 24, 29, 32–3, 68, 117–18
bird sanctuary 34
Blue Grotto 86
Blue Lagoon 77, 83, 84
bowling 22, 103
Bugibba 24–7, 110
buses 119–20
Buskett Gardens 86

C

Calypso's Cave 68, 69
car hire 114, 118
casinos 20, 25, 118
catacombs 62, 64
chemists 122
children 102–3
cinema 43
climate and seasons 115
Comino 8, 32, 76–81
Cominotto 8
Cospicua 51, 53–4
credit cards 114
crime and personal safety 124
cruises 11, 16, 51, 77, 83, 84–5
customs regulations 116

D

Dingli Cliffs 89
disabilities, visitors with 119
diving 11, 16, 22, 24–5, 34, 70–1, 105
drinking water 121
driving 114, 118, 119

E

eating out *see* individual locations
electricity 119

emergencies 123

F

festivals and events 106–7
Filfla 8, 89
food and drink 94–9

G

Ggantija 71
Ghajn Tuffieha 29, 32
Ghar Lapsi 89
glass-making 15, 100
Gnejna Bay 32
Golden Bay 29, 32
Gozo 8, 11, 32, 66–75

H

Hagar Qim 89
handicrafts 10, 43, 74, 100
health 120
helicopter tours 83–4
horse racing 105
horse riding 29, 102, 104

I

insurance 115, 121
Internet access 121

J

jeep tours 71

L

lacemaking 74, 100
lidos 20, 24, 34, 89
luzzus (fishing boats) 80

M

Malta Classic Car Collection 25
Malta Experience 11, 42
Maltese Cross 40
Marfa Ridge 32
marina 11, 20
markets 100
Marsalforn 67, 71
Marsaxlokk 78

Mdina 10, 56–61, 110
Mdina Dungeon 60, 103
medical treatment 121
Mellieha 32–6, 111
menu decoder 98
Mgarr Shelter 29–30
Mistra Bay 29
Mnajdra 89
money 114
Mosta Dome 11, 78, 80

N
Nadur 67
newspapers 121
nightlife *see* individual locations

O
opening hours 122

P
Paceville 20–3, 111
Paradise Bay 32, 33
passports and visas 114, 116
Portomaso 11, 20
post offices 123
prehistoric sites 29, 30, 71, 81, 89
public holidays 123

Q
Qawra 24–7, 110

R
Rabat 62–5
Ramla Bay 32, 33
religion 124
Roman baths 30
Roman villa 64

S
sailing 34
St George's Bay 20
St Julian's 20–3, 111
St Paul's Bay 28–31, 111–12
St Paul's islands 8, 29

Salina Bay 24
Senglea 51, 54–5
shopping 16, 43, 74, 100–1, 122
Skorba Temples 30
Sliema 14–19, 112
speedboats 84
sports centre 104
Sweethaven Village 35

T
Ta' Qali 10, 100
Tarxien Temples 81
taxis 120
telephones 124
theatre and concerts 42, 108
Three Cities 50–5
time differences 124
tourist information 113–14
traveller's cheques 114

U
Underwater Safari cruises 85

V
Valletta 10, 38–49, 83
Victoria 67, 72–3
Vittoriosa 51, 52–3

W
walking 105
water parks 102–3
watersports 11, 16, 20, 22, 24–5, 33, 34, 70–1, 105
wineries 90–2

X
Xaghra 67
Xemxija 29
Xlendi 67

Z
Zebbug 67

ACKNOWLEDGEMENTS

We would like to thank all the photographers, pictures libraries and organisations for the loan of the photographs reproduced in this book, to whom copyright in the photograph belongs:
David Browne (pages 28, 41, 103, 109); Emanuel Delicata (page 91); Pictures Colour Library (pages 37, 55, 96); Thomas Cook Tour Operations Ltd (pages 1, 5, 9, 13, 18, 22, 33, 44, 57, 69, 70, 75, 79, 80, 82, 85, 87, 93, 101, 104, 107, 108); World Pictures (pages 10–11, 26, 63, 76, 88, 94, 99).

Project editor: Catherine Burch
Layout: Trevor Double
Proofreader: Janet McCann
Indexer: Marie Lorimer

Send your thoughts to
books@thomascook.com

- Found a beach bar, peaceful stretch of sand or must-see sight that we don't feature?
- Like to tip us off about any information that needs a little updating?
- Want to tell us what you love about this handy little guidebook and more importantly how we can make it even handier?

Then here's your chance to tell all! Send us ideas, discoveries and recommendations today and then look out for your valuable input in the next edition of this title.

Send an email to the above address or write to:
HotSpots Series Editor, Thomas Cook Publishing, PO Box 227, Coningsby Road, Peterborough PE3 8SB, UK